What people are saying about Breastless Intimacy:

"Cynthia Friedlander's powerful writing chronicles her process, thoughts, but mainly her feelings as she finds her way through each new chapter of her life. Her insights are extremely helpful. I hope she will keep writing."
Renee Landau, Breast Cancer Survivor

"Breastless Intimacy is brilliant and heartfelt, written with pure, raw honesty and concern for all other beings."
Margot Bigge, Bilateral Mastectomy Breast Cancer Survivor

"I know how valuable it is for women to learn from others' experiences to help inform their decision-making process concerning mastectomy, implants and reconstruction. Cynthia Friedlander's memoir is an important contribution for women facing or having made choices regarding these difficult challenges."
Emilia Bulatt, Implant Consultant for
John E. Sherman MD FACS, specializing in reconstructive surgery

"Cynthia's poetic offering to the sobering and unromantic procedures of a bi-lateral mastectomy is soothing and validating. Her work connects us."
Jackie Shenkman, Breast Cancer Mastectomy Survivor and
Patient Advocate

"... Written in a clear, determined voice, each piece stands alone, ... Ranging from poetic prose to reflective musings, the writing is open and honest. ...

An illuminating collection of writing that's full of introspection and emotional transcendence."
Kirkus Reviews, Kirkus Media LLC

BREASTLESS INTIMACY

A Celebration of Love, Loss and Learning

... about being whole and desirable with significant scars and missing body parts

Cynthia Leeds Friedlander

Also by Cynthia Leeds Friedlander

Speak Easy, The Communication Guide for Career and Life Success (2009)

Breathe Easy, Letting Go of Expectation (2014)

On Butterfly Wings (Poetry)

Visit www.breastlessintimacy.com to order additional copies

To contact the author for speaking engagements:
info@clfconsultingservices.com

Giving...

This book is for

- My sister, Jodie, who never had the pleasure, before or after breast cancer, of fully experiencing wholeness, sensuality, sexuality and ultimate intimacy with a man she truly loved.

- Joy and all those other very young women who experience the ravages of mastectomy and breast surgery, before their lives have blossomed into the sexual fullness of mature womanhood.

- All those women facing or living with scarred and less than physically complete breasts.

- The sexual partners, friends and family members of women with altered bodies because of breast cancer.

- All those who question their desirability and feel less than whole in their sexual relationships and with their love partners.

Thank You...

Thank you, Emily, for writing the pain of your life openly, amusingly and honestly, and by doing so, revealing clearly to me how to take my love of writing and create what would be most meaningful to me and I hope to many others.

Thank you, Jesse, for going with me where we went together and for leaving me once again on the path alone. Being with you brought the birth of the concept for this book but it was your needing to pull away from me that provided the catalyst to make this happen.

Thank you, Kate, for believing in my writing and encouraging me to go to the next step.

Thank you, Iris, for your unselfishness and time; you gave your support and guidance asking nothing in return.

Thank you, Jennifer, for your honesty, wisdom and vision.

Thank you, Barry, for bringing me full circle and for believing in my writing and in me.

Thank you, Nate, for still and always being there. Your love, support and belief in me are the guiding lights in my life.

Thank you, Robin, for contributing your gifted creative and design vision to the look of Breastless Intimacy.

Thank you, brilliant authors, who paint with language and express so profoundly and magnificently what I can only glimpse in my own writer's eye and what I profoundly worship in the presence of your words.

Cynthia Leeds Friedlander

For Mother...

Life is about

-- hope and humor

-- loss and learning

-- making lemonade from lemons

and

-- seeing the magnificence to be found in the midst of the terror of human existence.

Cynthia Leeds Friedlander

"Security is mostly a superstition. It does not exist in nature, nor do the children of men as a whole experience it. Avoiding danger is no safer in the long run than outright exposure. Life is a daring adventure or nothing."

--- Helen Keller (1880 -1968)

Cynthia Leeds Friedlander

This is a book from my heart. I have written it as a gift, as a celebration of love, loss and learning. It's a book for those who are making, or have made, decisions to alter their bodies and are dealing with intimacy after those alterations. I recognize that it's less likely to be a book for those who are suffering or have suffered from advanced breast cancer and its many terrifying treatments. I watched my sister go through that end of the breast cancer spectrum and made choices to protect myself from those nightmares.

With the advances of genetics and medical technology, women have many more options and decisions to choose from than ever before. I made difficult choices in 1992 and again twenty years later in 2012 that were right for me and I have decided to share my experiences with others. Since my four-surgery year in 1993, I have been struck by the fact that many women have a variety of physical, emotional and medical reactions and problems that they often feel uncomfortable describing to anyone. Recognizing how easy it is for me to express what I need and want to say, I have developed a sense of desirable obligation to reveal openly what I have gone through. By describing a wide variety of my experiences, from flossing my teeth and shaving under my arms, to having a wire placed inside my breast, to placing my naked implanted breasts against a man's hairy chest for the first time after my surgery - I can provide a mirror for others to validate their own experiences and to open up a whole new world of perspectives, possibilities and adventures for them.

Breastless Intimacy *is a series of vignettes. Each one is written so that it stands alone and can be read in any order or as a single separate piece. The book is divided into four sections:*

(1.) ***My Bowls, Origins*** *and* ***Farewell*** *reflect my physical journey through life in relation to my breasts and their loss.*

(2.) ***Influence and Identity*** *and* ***Men and Breasts, Remembrances*** *celebrate encounters with men and what I learned from each.*

(3.) ***To Life*** *and* ***Messages*** *speak out to the world to be strong and vigilant in the face of danger.*

(4.) ***Full Circle*** *is an epilogue, written almost fifteen years after the prior three sections were written. It describes the shock of experiencing a failed and wilted saline breast implant twenty years after my original reconstructive surgery and the full circle and relationships in my life at that time.*

BREASTLESS INTIMACY: *A Celebration of Love, Loss and Learning*

Cynthia Leeds Friedlander

My Bowls

Cynthia Leeds Friedlander
My Bowls (1998)

Bowls, I call them my bowls. Even Jim, the surgeon who built
them for me, says they are not right:
    - too far apart, too high,
    - with noticeable ridges that look a bit
        like deep stretch marks
        as a result of insufficient saline fill,
    - too round and unnaturally shaped,
    - rather faded small circles of color
        with barely raised nipple mounds,
    - beyond young and perky,
        hard and stationary,
                no jiggling at all…
    - my bowls.

Jim wants to give me the newer ones that are tear-shaped and more
natural looking; my round bowls and bony ribcage reflect badly on
him and his reconstruction reputation, his artistry, his ego. He
wants me to be satisfied with how I look. I am satisfied. After
five years, they and their surrounding scars (which are finally
beginning to fade and soften somewhat) are the *new normal*. If it
weren't for the Polaroid photos of the *old normal*, taken in the
privacy of a sweet little house in the country just prior to their
removal, I would truly not even remember what the old ones
looked and felt like:
    - soft and low, falling out to my sides
    - with pale, almost imperceptible, silvery stretch marks
        from nursing my son
           from gravity
                from aging
    - and deep dark inky color widely
        encircling large button nipples.

Growing up, I often heard my grandmother say, "From the
moment you first give birth, your life is forever changed. Nothing
can mold you more significantly than being a mother." With my
infant son's first breath, I instantaneously experienced the
profound transition that she had described to me. Eighteen years

later, I was told that I had breast cancer and motherhood became second place in most significant life-changing experiences. The diagnosis:

- Ductile Carcinoma In Situ, DCIS
- Stage zero
- Nothing systemic, no blood vessel or lymph node involvement
- No radiation, no chemotherapy
- No life threat

Even though that diagnosis was relatively innocuous in the wide range of potential breast cancer stages and severity, I still decided to have my breasts removed. Three months prior, I had attended my sister's funeral, following her valiant fight against a viciously virulent strain of metastatic breast cancer.

A short time after my breast removal surgery, I attended a symposium on breast cancer. Dr. L. said to me following the panel presentation by her and other recognized medical professionals in the limelight of breast cancer treatment, "Oh, you didn't have breast cancer; carcinoma in situ is considered a pre-cancerous condition. And there certainly was no reason for you to have had a mastectomy." Right, Dr. L., I could have just left those pre-cancerous calcifications where they were and waited to see if they progressed to the stage or type of breast cancer that my sister Jodie had died of such a short time before my own diagnosis. Right!

And I certainly could have kept my left breast that had not been diagnosed with carcinoma in situ at all. Julia M., the radiologist who read my mammogram and who I believed walked on water, had said to me, "We'll have to watch these calcifications in your other breast." … and I thought to myself, "I don't think so, Julia. I have no desire to go through this experience more than one time in my life; thank you very much!" I never wanted to hear a diagnosis of breast cancer again. I was forty-six years old and knew that somewhere down the road, the likelihood of reoccurrence had tremendous potential!

Autopsies of many older women, who have died of causes other than breast cancer, reveal carcinoma in situ that could have been in their bodies for years without progressing beyond this non life-threatening stage. Not all carcinoma in situ: microscopic non-palpable cancerous calcifications scattered/clustered within the milk ducts of the breast, necessarily progress to other stages.

For me, the decision to remove both of my breasts was the right one to make.

"Pre-cancerous" and "stage zero" were music to my ears. My only sister had just died of breast cancer, after a two and a half-year courageous but ultimately hopeless fight. Her diagnosis:
- Stage three+.
- Every lymph node positive, nineteen, I believe.
- Extremely aggressive virulent type of cancer cell.
- In addition to the large mass in her breast, there had been a tumor growing at the base of her neck that you could see getting bigger and bigger each day prior to mastectomy and chemotherapy.
- Life threatening; infinitesimal chance of long-term survival.

Jodie's breast reconstruction had provided the only positive element of her medical journey during those two and a half years. I had witnessed the ravages of Jodie's going through chemotherapy, wig shopping and total hair loss (twice), traditional and gamma knife radiation and all the many resultant side effects, misery and episodes. I had seen what one natural breast and one reconstructed implanted breast looked like side by side. My decision was easy. My decision was clear. It wasn't until later that I would endearingly begin calling my reconstructed breasts "my bowls".

Origins

Cynthia Leeds Friedlander

Origins

From my earliest memories, I can recall dreams of flight where I am soaring high in the sky looking down on vast, empty and peaceful landscapes far below. The power of these night reveries is unparalleled. There is no drug, no sensation and no experience that compares to my night flights. Awaking from sleep after these dreams has always brought a sense of awareness that is exceptional: I *know* I have been flying, *not* dreaming. Every fiber of my being is stimulated and alive. I am high. I am high on flight. I am high on life.

Breast cancer robbed me of these dreams and their high for awhile. It was as if my power to soar had been stolen from me. Six years after my sister's death from breast cancer and five years after my own diagnosis and four-surgery year, the flying dreams blessedly and slowly returned. In my post-cancer dreams, my flight is no longer supremely high and the landscapes below are more complex, city-like and populated. Yet it is still quite heavenly that I have returned to flying.

Viscerally, I claim that these nocturnal flights began with birth, but perhaps they were actually Peter Pan inspired. I thrilled to his adventures as a little girl and believed, to the deepest core of my being, in the power of pixie dust and lovely thoughts to free the body from the earth. When we played Never-Never Land, I wanted to be Peter Pan, not a secondary female character like Wendy. Even when I grew too old for make-believe, my soul clung to faith in human flight while, ironically, I developed a fear of airplane flight that was equally intense. And most of all, like Peter Pan, I always knew the treasure of being a child. I never wanted to grow up.

When my contemporary girlfriends first began wearing high heel shoes and stockings, and started to shave their legs, I wanted to keep wearing short white socks with my patent leather ankle-strapped Mary-Jane shoes. I watched my cousin, Lonnie, who was a year older than I was, to see if she was still playing with her dolls. As long as she was, then I would have at least one more year to play with mine, one more year to be a child. Whenever I rode the bus across Wasena Bridge, I would savor moments of ordinary time and hold on to them with all my heart, as if by doing so I could stop time and be a child forever.

There were five granddaughters in the family, and no grandsons, when my mother became pregnant with me. A war had just ended and a boy baby was my grandfather's golden dream. Somehow a betting pool was started up and down the East Coast and wages were placed on whether Mr. D. would finally have a grandson. In small Southern towns, everyone knows the scoop about everyone else, so the nurse standing behind my mother's shoulders at my birth, asked immediately, "Is it a boy?" The doctor replied, "Yeah, it's a boy; it's a WAC." The nurse, having heard "whopper" rather than W(omen's) A(rmy) C(orps), ran to tell my father that he had a son. My father called all over town and to far away friends and relatives. Bets were collected and my grandfather wept for joy; he finally had his grandson. When my father was shown his new naked baby, who quickly kicked away the wrapping blanket, he exclaimed, "What the hell kind of boy do you call that?" Over the years, the story would be told many times in our family. And even though I would be referred to by my parents as their "little girl" well into my middle age, Daddy would often tell people that for a couple of hours he had a son or would ask them if they wanted to meet his little boy.

Growing up in a small Southern town surrounded by the Blue Ridge Mountains of Virginia, I felt protected from harm. Life was certainly sheltered in that place referred to as "The Star City of the South". When I first studied geography and learned that those mountains were barriers to hurricanes and tornadoes, I thought I was quite blessed to be living in such a guarded place. I could see those blue mountains from any vantage point in my Star City and always felt watched over by them. Each day when I left my house to go to school, my eyes would rest on my mountains and I would feel safe. When I first lived away from home, at college in Greensboro, North Carolina, I would walk out of the dorm each morning and have a split second of physical terror: "Where were my protective mountains?"

When I was around eight years old, my cousins were given a bicycle with training wheels. It was shiny new and alluring and I decided to try to ride it. Somehow I fell against the bar that I was straddling and injured myself rather severely. I was embarrassed to tell anyone of my vaginal pain, which was extreme. One of my older cousins found me crying in the bathroom later and helped me tell my parents about my injury. I was rushed to the doctor and the examination was so humiliating that I totally erased it from my memory. From then on, I would refuse to ride a boy's model bicycle, even though there would remain only hazy memories of the extreme bruising and horrible burning sensation from that fall. And it would not be until I was in high school, that my mother would tell me that there were pediatric medical records documenting that I had lost my hymen to that bicycle.

In that time before birth control pills, hippydom, Free Love, Civil Rights uprisings and the Women's Movement, the emphasis on virginity for girls, and the many double standards that went with it, provided codes for behavior that were clear and powerful. Being a "Good Girl" had so many layers to it. There were social pressures and familial ones that defined my choices, so that even with a medically recorded technical loss of virginity, I still followed the rules and moral codes of my generation regarding sexual intercourse before marriage.

Preoccupation with appearance is a common denominator of puberty, adolescence and early adulthood. Since my parents were both strikingly beautiful, I inherited my looks from both of them. People who had grown up with my mother would always tell me how much I looked like her and would always let me know that her beauty was incomparable. The physical appearance of my body was average with the only exception being that I was always rather thin. Having those wonderful physical attributes did not save me from the growing pains that everyone goes through and I never told anyone about the following:

    -Even though I had loved my childhood and wanted to prolong it, I was ashamed that all of my friends had started menstruating and I had not. In gym class, before I entered menses, I would answer the role "Reporting" once a month to indicate I had my period and would need to have reduced activity.

-I placed tissue in my bra to make my breasts appear bigger so that I would look as mature and sexy as my blossoming young girlfriends. I did not want to have big breasts but I wanted to be attractive to boys.

-I shaved under my arms when there was no hair at all there to try to stimulate its growth and in some way enhance my budding womanhood.

-In college, I spent hours in the library, trying to find out if there was something abnormal about my external vaginal appearance, since parts seemed to be growing and emerging that had not shown before.

My only sibling, Jodie, was seven years older than I was. Watching her struggle through life, I learned how *not to be*. Everything was hard for Jodie. She seemed to antagonize others naturally, with no malice in her heart. People experienced her intense curiosity as invasive and judgmental. In contrast, I was born full of endearment, knowing how to please everyone, with an ease that flowed out of me like song from a singer with perfect pitch. I was so engaging that I would confidently say to everyone, as I hugged and kissed them, "You love me, dontcha?" As an adult, I would find it embarrassing, but also sweet, to be reminded of that question which always rolled from my lips when I was a small girl.

Jodie hated me from the day I was born. I had invaded her complete world where she had been the center of attention and the sole recipient of parental affection for seven years. It would take a long time for us to have a true and sisterly love for each other. Jodie needed to be a wife and mother before she could see who I was, before she could love me without resentment for my invasion into her domain and for how effortlessly I connected to people and won their affection.

Over the years I developed a sense of self, a pride in my body and a confidence in my relationships that were in direct opposition to my sister:

> -She was the bad girl. I was the good girl.
> -She was the one that antagonized people. I was the one that pleased people.
> -She was fat. I was thin.
> -She was plain. I was pretty.
> -She was the one that fought the system. I was the one that espoused the system.
> -She was the one who exasperated our parents. I was the one who brought pride to our parents.
> -She was the one who married the wrong man. I was the one who married the right man. (The irony is that her marriage to Mr. Wrong lasted until her death and my excellent marriage to Mr. Right came apart and ended in divorce.)

When I was in my thirties, a close friend from college died an excruciatingly painful death from breast cancer. When Jodie was in her forties, breast cancer stole the life of one of her favorite young colleagues at work, a mother with two young children. In both instances Jodie and I spoke at length of these tragedies that were happening to our friends and how we felt that we could not possibly face and deal with such horrendous nightmares. In these conversations, we both said with great admiration, respect and terror, "How do people deal with this? I know I could never cope with anything so horrible!"

And yet we had to. And yet we did.

When Jodie first told me many years later about the suspicious mass that had been discovered in her breast, I felt like I had been transported to some foreign land where nothing was familiar. Jodie had nursed two babies, which was supposed to provide protection from breast cancer. There was no breast cancer, no cancer of any type, in our family. This happened to other people. It couldn't be happening to my sister.

For the next two and a half years I watched my sister fight a valiant but hopeless fight against her attacker.

- -I was by her side after biopsy surgery, when the surgeon first told her she had breast cancer and I then listened to her hysterical cries of terror, "I don't want to die in pain!"
- -I went with her to buy new nightgowns for the hospital before her mastectomy operation.
- -I helped her choose a wig and saw the tears streaming down her face as she looked in the mirror, wearing it for the first time.
- -I took her for chemotherapy treatments and sat across from her while those poisonous chemicals dripped into her veins.
- -I listened to the plastic surgeon describe reconstructive surgery to her and witnessed the unfolding of her subsequent breast reconstruction.
- -I took the hair from her head, the second time she lost it, and put it in a bag to keep forever.
- -I had photographs of everyone she loved, including her dog, photocopied and blown up, to place on the walls of her hospital room for her last birthday.
- -I lived through and shared each ordeal she suffered, one day at a time.

When I learned three months after my sister's funeral that I had a non life-threatening form of breast cancer in my right breast, I felt like the luckiest woman on earth. Like other extreme differences that had come to pass so many times in our lives, the contrast between our two original diagnoses was vast. Unlike Jodie, for me there was no lymph node or blood vessel involvement and neither chemotherapy nor radiation would be needed. When mastectomy was recommended to me as a result of the type and location of my breast cancer, in spite of the extremely early stage of cancer that I had, I chose, without hesitation, to remove and reconstruct both breasts simultaneously. Having lived through and witnessed my sister's battles in such a firsthand way, I wanted to protect myself from ever hearing another breast cancer diagnosis. I also had much knowledge and *inside* experience about breast cancer on which to base my decisions. If my sister had not been diagnosed with advanced breast cancer and recently died from it, my decisions and reactions would have been dramatically different. Even after death, Jodie was still the reverse role model for decisions I made and for how I wanted my life to be different from hers.

Often when I told others about my radical decisions, I would see the disbelief in people's eyes, as I would describe how easy it was for me to make the choice to have both of my breasts removed. I could feel women recoil at my conclusion. I saw their fear and loss of sexual self-image as they struggled with their own personal feelings about having to face such decisions. Many would convey to me, through facial expression alone, how strange they found my choices and my attitude. Others would challenge my decision outright. And some would begin to talk about how critical their breasts were to them for their sexual identity or in their sexual activity. I always understood and accepted their reactions and my convictions always remained solid, as I thought of my sister's suffering and death and of the assertive claim to life that I made in tribute to her.

And so it came to be that my sister and I, who experienced no sisterly love growing up, would develop that love in adulthood. We would find the friendship and mutual respect we never found as girls. We would become deeply bonded in later life and even after death, through our extremely opposite breast cancer journeys.

Farewell

Cynthia Leeds Friedlander
Good Bye, Dear Sister

My boyfriend and I had just returned from skiing in Utah. It had been close to seventy degrees at Sundance and there had still been great snow near the end of March. My face was deeply bronzed from the sun for the first time since my husband, my son and I had moved back to New York from Nassau, over thirteen years prior. Since then I had used sunscreen, a visor and dark protective sunglasses. The sun that I had always worshipped had become an enemy. It had been too glorious in Sundance and I had skied in only my cornflower blue/purple racing suit - without a ski jacket and without the sun visor.

When I arrived home from that splendid trip, there was an extremely disturbing message on my answering machine: "Cindy, please call me as soon as you get this message. I went to get a mammogram today and they sent me immediately to a surgeon's office to make an appointment for a biopsy. They said there is a suspicious mass in my left breast. I have been having pain in my arm and armpit, remember? I am terrified. Call me; please, *please* call me."

And so it began. Two and a half years of terror. Two and a half years of suffering. Two and a half years of hell.

Throughout my life, all I had to do was watch what my sister Jodie did and I would know what not to do. Growing up, she seemed to know exactly what would antagonize people and often did it, with no intention of harm or annoyance to others or the desire to generate inevitable ill will towards herself. As an adult I would come to appreciate how so much of what caused her problems came from her intense curiosity: Why? Why? Always and endlessly WHY! Her stubbornness and independent views coupled with almost zero awareness of other people's reactions certainly contributed significantly to how she often became her own worst enemy. Many times she would take a basic truth and turn it into an entire complex distorted concept which she would cling to like a religious tenet that her very soul's existence depended on:

Jodie was in her bedroom lying on one side of the king size bed she shared with her husband. Because of the toll of that day's course of chemotherapy, she had felt quite weak and had left the dinner table to lie down. I had brought her food to her and was stretched out on the other side of the bed to keep her company. I had found a "Time" magazine on the night table next to her husband's side of the bed and I was thumbing through it. "I didn't know you were a Republican." she calmly and confidently commented to me. "What gave you that idea?" I answered, somewhat shocked or at least baffled by her remark. "Well, W. (her husband) says that 'Time' magazine is a Republican magazine and I see you're reading it so...you must be a Republican, right?" Sometimes I just didn't want to challenge that kind of thinking. I said nothing.

Jodie's approaches to life actually came from a wonderful innocence and trust in the entire world, not from stupidity or even from a lack of the ability to think logically or critically. Jodie was quite intelligent. She loved every kind of complex puzzle, riddle, math problem, game and conundrum of any type. She was a superb bridge player and would spend hours with her son playing backgammon. She had designed complicated needlepoint and knitting projects, requiring amazing attention to miniscule details. When she went back to school in her forties, she excelled academically and could never learn enough. If she had lived a full life, she would never have stopped learning and growing professionally.

That trust she had in the world, rendered her gullible and often robbed her of logic and critical thinking. I could say with confidence that my sister never told a lie in her life. She simply was incapable of it. For the sake of honesty she would blurt out the truth at others' or her own expense, without even realizing the damage she was doing. The truth was the truth and she could not see beyond that. The impact of her words was foreign to her. She was unaware, quite unsophisticated and terribly naïve. She never lied and she assumed that no one ever lied to her.

Jodie had been an only and adored child for seven years before my birth. She absolutely loathed me from the day I was born. And why not! I had invaded her realm.

> When Jodie was about eight years old, she went to our father, sobbing and terrified. "What's the matter, Jodie darlin'?" my father asked. "Oh, Daddy, I'm so scared." "What are you scared of, sweetie?" "I want to kill Cindy and I'm so afraid that I will do it." My father took her into his arms and hugged her tightly to his chest. "Jodie, honey, you never have to be afraid that you're going to kill your baby sister. If you were really going to kill her, you would have never told me about it. You don't have to be frightened of these feelings. They're perfectly normal feelings to have."

It would take years and years for love to grow between Jodie and me.

I was born with the gift of knowing exactly what to do and to say to please everyone. In addition to my innate awareness and affectionate nature, I had Jodie to watch as a reverse role model. The good child/bad child syndrome was fertilized and flourished in our home.

At the age of three, I would stand at my big sister's side, tugging at her skirt, and beg her to stop antagonizing our parents. "SHHHHHHH, Jodie. *Please* don't say *anything*. Just listen to them and tell them they're right. Please, don't talk back anymore. You're going to get in so much trouble! Jodie, *please*." But she never could be quiet. Even when there was a no-win situation, she had to express whatever she was thinking. And to add insult to injury, she had to put up with a pleading three-year-old, begging her to change her behavior.

Many years later, soon after I became separated from my husband, I traveled alone to Smith Mountain Lake, Virginia, near where I grew up, to visit my parents and in particular to spend time with my father who was recuperating from an angioplasty procedure. My young son had been there with them for several days and so had my sister and her husband. When at last I arrived, my mother was so concerned about me. She focused intensely on my driving alone, my emotional well being, my fatigue from the trip. It was as if no one else on earth existed - not my father who had just had quite a medical scare and not my older sister who was also deserving of that same kind of mother love and attention.

Later that evening, practically in the dark, I was showing my sister how to clean the striped bass she had caught in the lake that day. She was the only one among us to catch a fish and it was definitely a keeper. She was so happy. I had taught my father and her to fish and she had come to share my deep enthusiasm for the sport. We were in the kitchen, trying not to get blood and guts all over the place, which would have definitely upset our mother. It was quite amusing carrying out this clandestine activity in the middle of the house in semi-darkness. Suddenly, my brother-in-law, who was observing us, asked my sister how she could stand the way I was treated. He asked Jodie why she didn't hate me. I would never ever forget my sister's answer. We had grown close as adults and in particular in those years when my sister gained self-esteem through her education and occupational therapy career. Her life had truly blossomed as she gained confidence and perspective that she had not had as a girl or young woman. When she answered her husband that night in the middle of that semi-lit kitchen with fish guts and slime all over the counter, I loved her with all of my heart. "Don't you know how hard that is for Cindy? She's the one who has all the pressure, not me!"

My sister's biopsy surgery was done with only local anesthesia. The surgeon came out of the out-patient operating room to tell my brother-in-law and me exactly what the initial frozen section had shown. My sister definitely had breast cancer. He asked us to come into the O.R. with him to tell my sister what they now had confirmed. It was a horrific experience. Jodie was hysterical and terrified. She kept screaming over and over, "Oh no, oh no! I don't want to die in horrible pain." I made a promise to her that I could not have kept and fortunately never had to face, "I promise you, Jodie, you will not die in pain." My thoughts were totally focused on assisted suicide and I knew that if it were to become necessary, I would help my sister end her life.

The night before Jodie's mastectomy, her two grown children slept on the floor of her bedroom on either side of their parents' bed. Jodie sobbed, moaned and cried out all night long. I was staying in a room down the hall and slept intermittently as her shrieking fear and sadness tore me from of my restless sleep. There were five of us in the car the next morning to take Jodie to have her breast removed. Paul McCartney was singing, 'Let It Be" on the radio as we approached the hospital, and my niece, nephew, brother-in-law and sister sang out the chorus as if it were a battle hymn. "Let it be. Let it be." They heard the lyrics as an omen of survival. I heard them as a message to accept the coming of death. "And in my hour of darkness, Mother Mary comes to me, speaking words of wisdom; let it be, let it be."

Jodie's breast cancer eventually metastasized to her brain so there gratefully was no pain, only a slow paralysis of her entire body, a gradual incoherence and loss of being in touch with reality, and eventually a coma which lasted for weeks because of her strong heart and otherwise healthy body.

There were many wonderful and precious times Jodie and I shared that have provided me with lasting, beautiful and simple memories to be cherished forever:
-The trip to Nassau.
-My head under the sofa pillow, to hide from the older kids, wisely knowing that I was still in view.
-An autumn afternoon spent fly fishing with golden sunlight filtering down through the trees.
-Insisting that Jodie leave the movie, "Snow White", to take me home, because I was frightened.
-Sharing a picnic of steamed artichokes and eggplant parmesan.
-Elegant lunches at the High Lawn Pavilion.
-Fishing for fluke from "Seas the Moment" in Reynolds Channel.

-Sharing the piano bench, playing *Chopsticks* and *Heart and Soul.*

-Making bedroom curtains together at the sewing machine, side by side.

-Lunch at Bienvenu with Edward.

-Our grandmother's piano.

-Jodie's teaching me to knit when I was eight years old.

-Dogs, dogs, dogs, dogs, dogs.

-Rolling Jodie's hospital bed in front of the window to show her the Fourth of July fireworks.

-Jodie's joy on her last birthday when I filled her hospital room with huge photos of everyone she loved.

-The Rodin exhibit in Philadelphia.

-The George Winston concert at Lincoln Center.

-The play, "Night Mother".

Good bye, dear and only sister. I so hope you are with Mamaw, serenely playing duets on the piano. Your children have built such wonderful lives for themselves. Your grandchildren are delicious. Rest in peace.

Cynthia Leeds Friedlander
Bravery, Jubilance and Terror

Feeling jubilance and terror simultaneously can be somewhat wearing but also rather exciting. There are certainly only a small number of experiences as frightening as receiving a diagnosis of cancer. I first learned of this dreaded disease as a little girl, when a good friend's mother was diagnosed with breast cancer. Cancer meant Death. People didn't talk openly about cancer in those days and no one thought of survival when hearing the "C" word. I went to bed terrified the night I learned of her illness. Shortly thereafter I started adding the words, "Don't let me think of bad things; don't let me have bad dreams and please let me die in my sleep" to the ritual prayer that I repeated to God every night when I went to bed. How could there be such a terrifying disease that there was no cure for?! I couldn't bear thinking about it.

When the radiologist, Julia M., read my mammogram that day in December of 1992 and told me with confidence that what she saw was certainly going to be revealed through biopsy as cancer, I somehow felt totally calm. She was extremely reassuring that this was not going to kill me, knowing that I had just lost my sister to breast cancer. This was microscopic. This was what they always "recommended": EARLY DIAGNOSIS!

My cousin, Harry, was in town on a business trip that day and he provided tremendous loving support. I ended up going to see the Alvin Ailey Dance Company at the City Center that night as planned with a friend, staying calm, thrilling to the beauty of the performances as always and also becoming somewhat dazed and numb as those in shock often do. I kept waiting to wake up from the nightmare I was in, but it was no dream. It was real. I had breast cancer.

The next few days required choosing a breast surgeon/oncologist. The first one I saw had removed a benign fibroid tumor from my left breast when I was thirty-four. He was a marathon runner and since I was so athletic and loved running, I had felt comfortable with him previously and thought I would feel the same way at this significantly more critical point in time. It turned out to be quite

36

fortuitous that he could not get me on his surgery schedule until January, prompting me to make an appointment with another surgeon.

The difference in how these two physicians provided information and interacted with me was amazing. The first one, the runner, withheld much information, answered my questions in a cursory manner and basically spoke to me as if I had little or no ability to understand much or to make an appropriate decision. The second one gave me a lot of information detailing what I had and, although clear in his recommendations, still had a two-way dialogue with me and answered questions endlessly, incorporating my needs and individual preferences into alternatives. I left his office with an appointment for the biopsy even later in January than the other surgeon's first available date. And I also left there jubilant. It seemed to me that I was the luckiest woman on earth. No chemotherapy, no radiation! No threat to my life! I had watched my sister deal with and succumb to the devastation of virulent metastatic breast cancer. I was ecstatically alive and knew in so many ways -- that I wished I had never learned of -- that this was going to be *relatively* easy.

The doctor had told me that if calcifications were found in the margins (outermost edges) of the biopsy tissue, then he would recommend mastectomy. He told me that because there are a tremendous number of ducts throughout the breast and because these calcifications were microscopic, that there was currently a consensus of opinion to remove the breast even though in other types of more advanced breast cancer, lumpectomy was most often the recommended route. He supportively discussed with me the concept of prophylacticly removing the other breast. He gave me clear statistics on a variety of scenarios. I left his office rejoicing and vigilant. I would live and I would choose aggressive measures to ensure my peace of mind and future health.

Those closest to me were shocked when the biopsy results led to a recommendation to remove my breast and were even more so when they saw how calm and even eager I was to proceed. The major shock of all to them was that I had chosen to make it a double breast ceremony. Off with the boobs! That was it for me. I was 100% clear and definite. There was zero ambivalence and zero reluctance. I knew what they were thinking: She's the sexy one. She's the physical one. She's still single and wants to be married. She is giving up that part of her sexuality, totally, when there is no reason. Why would she do that?! There will be double pain and recuperation. There is no reason to remove a healthy breast.

There were many reasons I was so easily able to make the decisions I made. Yes, for sure, the main driver was that I never ever wanted to hear a breast cancer diagnosis again or go through the same experience (or worse) in the future. But there was more: I was athletic and loved active sports. Boobs had always seemed to be extra "stuff" that kind of got in the way. I was glad mine had been fairly small, unlike my mother's, and actually wondered why so many men thought that big breasts were so appealing.

In contrast to this nonchalance about giving up my breasts, nursing my son had been among the greatest experiences of my life, and amusingly that loss felt the most painful for me. It was unlikely that I would ever be doing that again, but the loss of that capacity seemed enormously sad.

My strong sense of self provided the main reason that I could make those decisions so easily. I had always been sensual and sexual. I liked my body and cared a great deal about fitness and my body's appearance. Yet somewhere down deep inside me, I had always known that, even though I was blessed with physical beauty, my real beauty and sex appeal came from *who I was inside,* from my energy and playfulness, from my joie de vivre, from my clever brain and from my word-gifted tongue -- and not from my looks and definitely not from my breasts! And so, I could willingly and decidedly give them up. They were not who I was!

At some point during this highly demanding and stressful period, prior to the simultaneous mastectomy / reconstruction surgery date, I had an incredibly wonderful insight that served me enormously throughout that entire four-surgery year:

Stress/Fear = Excitement/Anticipation!
Excitement/Anticipation = Stress/Fear!

There were many moments when I felt sheer terror about what was in my body and what was going to happen to it surgically,
> -even though I constantly carried with me how different my breast cancer diagnosis was from my sister's,
> -even though I had my close friend's ears and memory (from her being with me at all of my doctors' appointments) to reconfirm exactly what those doctors had all said about the non-life-threatening stage of breast cancer that I had,
> -even though I had a biopsy report stating "stage zero" in black and white.

I began to analyze all of the components of my fear as if it were some force outside of me. At the same time I became totally aware of how similar each of those components was to the exact reactions I would experience when I was joyfully excited and full of anticipation about some wonderful event or circumstance. They felt identical to me in every way: the breathing, the heart rate, the adrenaline rush. So I consciously decided that I was going to be excitedly anticipatory about each of the hurdles that lay ahead, since the emotions were all readily accessible to me through my fear anyway. And I *was* exuberant and proud of how well I was handling such major stuff.

Not a day went by that I didn't think about the following:
> -When my sister had been forty-six years old, (as I was at the time of my diagnosis) mammography equipment was not sophisticated enough to show the type of microscopic in situ calcifications that were later identified in my breast at stage zero.
> -I would never know if her breast cancer started in the same way or at the same age as mine.

-I was exceedingly fortunate to be seven years younger
than she was.

These thoughts provided a sense of sadness for my sister and of
anticipatory excitement about my future.

Many people said to me that I was incredibly brave and showed
such wonderful courage in the face of adversity. I felt surprised at
their comments and couldn't imagine exactly what they were
observing. What choice was there, anyway? Kicking and
screaming? Putting my head in the sand? Trembling in my boots?
(That kind of terror was for airplane flights!) It was all so clear to
me. Jodie was the one to have been terrified. Jodie was the one
who needed bravery to confront all of her deathly challenges. I
just had to face four surgical procedures (with general anesthesia
all four times) in one year, along with some accompanying pain
and healing. I just had to gain some thick and ugly scar tissue as
souvenirs of my year of surgery. I just had to give up my breasts.
I just had to visit the plastic surgeon regularly to have my implants
expanded and my skin stretched. I just had to face a future
without hormone replacement therapy. It all seemed like easy
payment for my life. I had seen "the other side" and I didn't have
to go there. Bravery seemed easy, if even required at all.
Chemotherapy required bravery! Loosing every hair on your body
required bravery! Radiation required bravery! I had it easy! I
was rejoiceful! I became excited about what lay ahead. I had
much to anticipate but mostly *I had my future*.

There was one aspect to all of this that did require a great deal of
courage. Since my parents had been through two and a half years
of agony during my sister's illness and were no longer young and
resilient, I decided that I would not tell them about my diagnosis
and surgery until much further down the road. I knew it would
destroy them. Keeping everything from them then and finally
telling them all much later was going to be extremely challenging.
My parents were too old and too worn down to go through my
experience with breast cancer, no matter how much contrast there
would be to the horrors of my sister's ordeals. I also needed to
maintain my vigilance and excitement about the road ahead and
did not need to worry them or be pulled into their fears.

Since it was so critical to keep them totally unaware of what was happening, I was quite careful about whom I told of my situation. Those friends and family members closest to me were selectively informed and sworn to secrecy. This helped me keep a sense of privacy, which I cherished greatly, and of control, which was such a highly desirable commodity in the face of cancer.

Having accepted the mantle of courage and rejected the banner of bravery, I was also definitely able to continue to embrace my eternally optimistic view of life and that "Anne Frank belief" in the goodness that still exists when there is much to be terrified of everywhere. In our family we had always quoted my Aunt Hannah, "You don't have to like it; you just have to do it!" Life was full of so many ups and downs; learning to accept what couldn't be changed and going with the flow were simply basic survival necessities. Being able to see it all as a great adventure provided significant learning and powerful exuberance during the ride. Strangely, I would come to realize that I wouldn't take anything for what I gained from my experience with breast cancer. It would have been great to have learned all that I learned without such an experience. And that was exactly the point. The only way to gain that kind of learning was through the life-changing experiences I was living each day.

I knew, appreciated and deeply understood that and remained jubilant about life when there was much to fear and much to grieve.

Choosing the Breastmaker

It was important, fun and even catty having my friend, Rita, with me to listen to and evaluate breast reconstruction plastic surgeons as they provided information about surgical approaches that were required as a result of the disease in my body, about procedures to provide new breasts and about subsequent choices regarding the various options. Her friendship and support were immensely valuable to me. We almost always saw the world in the same way, even though our life choices and decision-making styles were often quite different. It was critical to have her eyes, ears, observations and perceptions along side of my own in this time of crisis and difficult decision making.

I had first met Rita years prior when she was a participant in the seminars I was running for women exploring reentry into the workforce. I remember how immediately struck I was by her eloquence as she participated in group discussions. I also recognized right away that I wanted her to be my friend. After the seminars were over, our friendship evolved slowly and eventually became family-like; our sisterly relationship was greatly enriching to both our lives.

In one of our visits to find my breastmaker, I sat topless on an examining table, with Rita and a nurse in the room, while the surgeon dictated his methods, actually using a purple magic marker to draw lines on my breasts exactly where he would be making incisions. It was humiliating. I felt violated. He informed me that prior to surgery, I would have to have my breasts photographed in a photographer's studio by some non-medical stranger, in spite of my vehemently expressing objections to such a dehumanizing procedure. Rita definitely reinforced my decision to reject this doctor in spite of how highly he had been recommended and, from that day on, she would always refer to him as "that arrogant prick".

Rita and I liked Jim immediately. He examined me alone in a small examining room. Then I dressed and sat down in his office with Rita, as he, with seemingly no time constraints, provided information, offered options and answered questions. He was shocked to hear about the other surgeon's drawing on my breasts and his insisting that cancer patients have their breasts photographed. Instead of showing me a book of photographs of his "work", as the other surgeon had, Jim asked if I would like to speak to and <u>see</u> other patients who wanted to share with, and "show" themselves to, newly diagnosed women facing hard decisions.

It was difficult to hear Jim reconfirm that I would have little feeling in the nerve endings of my reconstructed breasts and probably considerable numbness. And it was most difficult to be told again that I would definitely lose all sensation of sexual arousal derived from my breasts.

I asked him if after my surgery I could continue to wear the lycra stretch leotard type tops and knit camisoles that I was so comfortable wearing. I had always disliked wearing bras and found them to be constraining encumbrances and so had worn them as seldom as possible. It was then, as I described my need to look sexy and wear tight lycra stretched across my bralessness, that Rita began to ensure my sense of sexuality and sensuality by lovingly saying to me, "You're such a slut!", providing humor and lightness in a scary stressful time and reassuring me that I was and would still be sexy and desirable. Jim was kind enough to tell me that of course I would be able to wear those types of tops with my newly made breasts, without pointing out that my old sagging milk-stretched breasts were no longer primo for those garments anyway.

Jim also told me, as others had, that my only choice for breast reconstruction was saline implants since I did not have enough body fat for the kind of reconstructive surgery available to women using their own bodies to create much more natural-looking and feeling breasts. Several of my friends gladly offered to give me their excess body fat for this purpose. With appreciation and laughter, I refused their joking offers, since there were no surgical or medical advances to allow for this type of donation. Because these procedures were quite complex and time consuming, and

43

involved making additional incisions that would leave more scars, moving tissue and muscle from other parts of the body and reconnecting blood vessels, I would have rejected that type of option anyway. It felt good to know that I was too fit and lean for that choice.

It was easy to select Jim as my breastmaker. The process would provide the foundation for maintaining my sense of physical wholeness and sexuality after mastectomy. Making that choice gave me the feeling of control of my body that a cancer diagnosis can destroy. It was a way to maintain my desirability and avoid feeling victimized. The following words formed over and over in my head, "Thank you, Jim." "Thank you, Rita."

Rejection and Wholeness

Christopher Reeve's book, *I'm Still Here*, revealed what an incredible journey he had to make. His description of his accident, total paralysis and return to full life, even with his many losses and serious limitations, is moving. His writing about his wife and his marriage and how they found ways to share physical and sexual intimacy together in spite of what was missing and nonfunctioning is inspiring. Clearly, my no longer having natural functioning breasts would take nothing away from my identity nor from my sexuality. My sense of wholeness would remain intact and I would always be able to say, "I'm still here."

The night before my big surgery to remove and begin the reconstruction of my breasts, I was organizing my home and tying up loose ends, knowing I would not be fully functional for at least a couple of weeks. I had told only a selected few people about my diagnosis and future operations. Privacy was a critical ingredient in my life, even though I was always incredibly open and able to connect easily with the "entire world". When I had been pregnant with my son, I had hated how total strangers would ask me questions about my pregnancy. Knowing how well-meaning they were, I still wanted to tell them, "None of your business; I don't know you." instead of "The first week in June." or "A boy who looks just like his father."

There were people who knew my sister had just died after a grotesque battle with breast cancer. I knew that, if what I was going through became public, everyone would have me buried with my sister as soon as they heard the news, no matter how it was presented and no matter how different our diagnoses and prognoses were.

Of course, there was also the control factor; it was so clear to me that I wanted to control no one and I wanted to ensure that no one and nothing controlled me, except myself. Every chance I could find to keep control of my life, I seized wholeheartedly. So it was imperative that I limited who would know, and talk to me (or to others), about my upcoming breast removal event.

There were friends who were so easy to talk to – discreet, supportive, humorous, kind. It was so good to be able to share with them easily and know I could trust them, without worrying about their pity or their exposing my situation to others. There was one person with whom I was less comfortable and against my basic instincts, I decided to share my story with her.

Over the years, she had reached out to me several times collegially and personally, and I decided to set the stage for a more personal and open relationship with her, by telling her in confidence about my diagnosis and surgery. Although minor and inconsequential, it was the only decision during that time that I would come to regret.

That night she called me on the telephone and announced, "We will all be praying for you tomorrow and you know, it's not too late for you to change your mind about what you're doing." I said nothing and just sat there stunned, in silence and disbelief. "I've said the wrong thing, haven't I?" she asked. "Yes, you definitely have!" I replied. She continued on and on and made it much worse. It was shocking to hear her describing all of my surgery the next day as elective. She clearly couldn't handle the thought of my being able to give up my breasts. She wanted to comfort me by telling me that she knew that breast cancer is the worst possible experience for women, as prostate cancer is the worst for men. There was no comfort at all in these strangest of comments the night before my bilateral mastectomy surgery.

Managing my fear and keeping calm were my highest priorities, and there I was being jousted out of my tranquility and having to deal with that woman's fear. She was revealing her obsession with her own breasts and her own identity. How incredulous it was that she had been so insensitive! And how striking to see that a person could have so little sense of self and could gain so much of her identity from image and from physical sexual body parts.

The bizarre remarks made to me that night had a strong connection to another night and another shocking comment made many years before about a body part and identity. During a break in a rehearsal for a high school play, a group of us were sitting around talking about one of the teachers in the school who was devoutly religious and extremely biased against non-Christians. We began making sick jokes about her that evolved into a rather complex almost Nazi-like scenario where she would hunt down and exclude all Jews from any participation in public activities and they would be shipped off to some type of exiled existence. Several of my friends promised to hide and protect me from her. One of the girls in the group said to me, "Well, Cindy, you could always get a nose job." And I immediately, proudly and cleverly responded with my ever ready tongue, "Why would I want to do that? My nose has gotten me a lot further than yours has gotten you!" This was followed by applause from my friends and deep blushing from the girl.

These two comments, made so many years apart, each reflected how someone insecure had attached a personal identity to a body part - the Jewish nose, the female breast – which was totally misplaced and misrepresentative. Gratefully, in each instance, I knew viscerally and emotionally how disconnected my identity was to those body parts.

Knowing I was whole, and would remain so without breasts, made mastectomy an experience that I could conquer without any hesitation and with only minor but deep sadness.

It is who we are inside that carries us through the toughest losses and lets us come out on the other side stronger and better for the experience.

47

Surgery Behind Me: Buttfatnipples

Four general anesthesia experiences in one year was definitely beyond any quota I would ever have wanted to set for myself and so 1993 provided a wonderful opportunity for the ever famous "One day at a time!" approach:

Biopsy, January
Mastectomy/Reconstruction, February
Implant Exchange, May
Nipple Reconstruction, November

Biopsy, January : It was basically a "Now we're going to tell you what we've already told you." situation. Based on my desire, the amount of non suspicious but abundant calcifications in my breast tissue, and my sister's recent death from BC, it was decided to do a random biopsy of the left breast in addition to the right breast with the identified ductile carcinoma in situ. This would serve to add some potentially hard data to the decision making process. If mastectomy were to be recommended for the right breast, then perhaps I would choose a "two for the price of one" (well, not quite) benefit, or decide to keep that left breast for the time being and wait until a real need came later to remove it. I wanted to avoid that kind of possibility, *at any cost*.

My right breast, with the identified in situ calcifications, needed absolutely the opposite of random selection for the biopsy. What was required was locating and marking those microscopic calcifications in my right breast, so that the surgeon would know exactly what to remove for the biopsy. The process would perhaps be the worst experience of the whole year. Okay, the second worst. Bilateral mastectomy and reconstruction of both breasts in one surgical event would definitely win first place for worst experiences in 1993, no contest! The number two ranking directly related to how almost non-existent the calcifications were. Something needed to be removed that couldn't be seen by the naked eye. So how would the surgeon remove what couldn't be seen? It was certainly a pretty tricky concept. And even when the procedure was explained to me, prior to its being done, it was still difficult and frightening to imagine how it would be to go through such an experience. The only good part of that horrendous pre-op procedure was knowing I could make choices to ensure that I would never have to go through it again!

Marking the Microscopic

While the breast is in the mammography "press", a wire is inserted deep inside the breast and left there to mark the area that needs to be removed. The process requires a number of mammography views to be taken and reviewed to ensure that the wire is exactly where it needs to be so that the surgeon will know precisely what tissue to remove. The "press" can not be released until the entire procedure is completed. This may take anywhere from a half hour to an hour (or more). The first attempt to place the wire correctly is rarely exact. The wire is left inside the breast as a surgical marker. Even though local anesthesia is used, there is considerable discomfort. Unlike traditional mammography where the patient stands, the patient is seated in a chair for this procedure.

It was shocking to me when two years later a woman told me she was scheduled for this procedure and had not been told at all what was going to happen. When I realized that she was totally unprepared for what would take place, I felt a sense of obligation to prepare her for what she was going to experience. She actually became quite upset and expressed her anger toward me for telling her what would be done to her. She told me that she preferred to be uninformed and relaxed. I felt horrible that I had followed my instincts to enlighten her, when the breast surgeon had not felt such a need.

Later, she came back to me and thanked me for having told her what to expect, even though she had been so upset at the time that I had. She said, "Cindy, it would have been horrifying to have been subjected to that without any prior understanding of what it would be like. Thank you so much for what you did. I'm so sorry that I got angry with you."

When I went through that extremely unpleasant pre-op procedure, I certainly wanted to be informed and gain a sense of control and calm from knowing exactly what was going to happen to my body. I couldn't imagine how someone could choose to place herself totally in the hands of her physician and be as little informed as possible. It also seemed unethical and arrogant for a surgeon to schedule a woman for a procedure like that without thoroughly describing it to her beforehand.

Anesthesiologist #1 did not put me out prior to my being rolled into the operating room for the biopsy surgery, with that wire inside my breast. When I came into that cold and ominous room, lying on my back, there was a huge rush of totally unexpected emotion. I felt transposed into my sister's body and sensed her terror, hopelessness and desire to flee. My grief was enormous. It was so sad to think of how many times she went through anesthesia and surgery during her two-and-a-half-year ordeal, without the benefit of survival. Once again, as had happened over and over in our lives, she got the lousy outcome and I got the wonderful one. Joy, guilt and sorrow all welled up in me at the same time.

Mastectomy/Reconstruction, February : The second anesthesia was "the big one" and I should have been totally out of it until the next day at least. I had packed toiletry stuff and whatever I would need in the hospital in a small suitcase. Without my knowing it, my cousin and boyfriend had conferred while I was in surgery and decided to take the suitcase back home for the night, since I undoubtedly would not know what was happening, much less want whatever I had packed. I have no memory at all of the recovery room but do remember being moved from the gurney to my bed sometime in the early evening. Evidently, I must have been in excruciating pain but all that I remembered after was seeing my cousin, Lonnie, turn ashen, watching me as they put me in the bed.

The nurse I hired for this crucial time specialized in mastectomy surgery and had been highly recommended. I found her patronizing and coddling, not a particularly effective style with my personality. I wanted to floss and brush my teeth that night and was outraged that a decision had been made to take my bag home. The need to have a sense of normalcy and control was *huge* for me, even that closely on the heels of surgery. The nurse was "now-nowing" me as if I were a child and I was not going to be "now-nowed" at all. In the end, my dental floss and toothbrush were brought to me from home and I could begin to feel the way I needed, to get through the first of a few rather horrific nights.

The flossing thing was a real big issue for me. I had made a pact with God years before about my father's health. Somewhat childish, but it worked for me. Prior to my pact, I could never get myself to do this important dental activity. Since the pact, I had never missed a single night of flossing and that night was not going to be one of them. What great satisfaction I gained from being in control of what I did and of what happened to me. This basic trait contributed hugely to my being able to master an uncontrollable nightmare.

Implant Exchange, May: Anesthesia #3 was a relatively uneventful experience. It did, however, result in my finally having permanent implants, later to be fondly named my bowls. They were much more comfortable and appropriately sized for my frame.

Need for Exchange

The initial implant is temporary because it is designed to be expanded over time by adding saline, so that the skin can gradually stretch to its needed capacity for the size breast that is desired, much the same way the skin stretches during pregnancy. The interim implant is larger and bulkier than the permanent one will be, in order to extend the breast size beyond the final desired amount. This over stretching is done to increase the potential for the skin to "hang" more naturally later, thus creating a more normal breast appearance. The temporary implant is made with a slightly raised and thickened receptor/port area to receive the saline for expansion, which is another reason this initial implant is no longer needed or wanted after the breast is adequately filled out.

Prior to the implant exchange surgery, I remember telling Jim that I was having difficulty shaving under my arms with the temporary implants. In response to my shaving problem, Jim said that he had never heard anyone else say this and that he was completely unaware of such a problem with other patients. Over time, when I spoke to other women who had gone through this procedure, others told me they experienced the same shaving difficulty.

Nipple Reconstruction, November: Anesthesiology experience #4 had an unusual slice to it. The current anesthesia drugs were quite wonderful. Not only did they knock you out so that you couldn't feel anything at all, they also kept you from remembering the time frame when you were under and also the time just preceding and directly following as well. Even though the nipple reconstruction was done on an outpatient basis, which meant I had to be conscious, coherent and able to be released from the recovery room on my own steam, I had no memory of leaving the hospital that day or of how I got home. The first post-surgery memory I had was sitting in my own bed, eating a turkey sandwich. It was quite bizarre, though, because I did have some kind of distinct memory about body fat associated with the surgery. In the three preceding surgeries, I had remembered nothing, other than that first grief-filled entry into the operating room.

So when I went to see the surgeon for my first post-op appointment, I told him that I kept having this strange memory about body fat connected to my surgery and he began laughing, but was also rather surprised. "The reason you have that memory is that you didn't have any body fat at all in your chest area and I had to take it from your butt to make your nipples. We were definitely discussing it in the O.R., but you couldn't possibly have

actually heard this conversation or known what was happening."
He proceeded to take a piece of paper to illustrate the procedure;
with a small scissors he cut out an oval shape exactly like the
ellipses of skin that he took from the creases under my butt on
each side to make the areolas for my new nipples. Then he sliced
open the middle of the ellipse and rolled a central flap into a little
cylinder. He told me that this cylinder required fat to fill it up to
give it the appearance of a natural nipple and that he usually took
that fat from the chest area directly under where he placed the
ellipse. Since in my case there wasn't any chest fat at all, he had
to take it from my bottom where he had just removed the skin for
the areolas. We both laughed and shook our heads because neither
of us could understand how I knew about the body fat story.

Shortly after this last surgical event, a friend said to me, "Aren't
you glad that you have it all behind you finally?" and I answered,
"Well, actually what used to be behind me is now in front of me."

Cynthia Leeds Friedlander
Arousal: Nippleless Foreplay

There is no response to touch in my new nipples. If I scratch my fingernails across them, I can feel the slightest hint of pressure, which is truly more imaginary than actual. Basically they are numb. The surrounding skin also lacks sensation with the minutest gradual increase in feeling, moving concentrically outward from the nipples. In the outermost circle of skin that covers my implants and just before the flatness of my chest wall, I have normal feeling and can successfully scratch itches. There is no nerve path left at all to transmit sexual arousal. None.

I deeply mourn this loss of feeling in my breasts. Out of my sadness, I summon all of my memory to recreate that initial flow of sexual excitement. The capacity simply no longer exists. I laugh through my sadness when I suddenly feel that all of the effort to recapture this sensory memory has arrived at the appropriate lower destination anyway. It's somehow reminiscent of a game of Monopoly: Go directly to ... Do not pass GO. Do not collect $200.00.

When I had been told prior to surgery that I would lose all sexual sensation in my breasts, it didn't seem that important to me. My breasts had never been a central focus for me while making love. There were those big dark terra cotta nipples that stood at attention when stimulated, that I would be giving up, but my primary sexual focus was elsewhere.

And so at the end of the following year, when I was finally ready to venture out with my new breasts and begin the dance again, it was a grand surprise to me that I felt so deprived of this starting place. I simply had never realized the extent to which new sexual beginnings depend on nipples - so easily available, immediately responsive and innocent in their accessibility. They were not there anymore to set the stage for what comes next or even provide a sexual destination of their own.

There was also the unhappy realization that I had lost the wonderful distraction from the "main event" that nipples provided.

I no longer had an alternate stimulation focus to aid in the delicious delay of sexual zenith.

When I was in college, I had a close friend who was dating an older guy, probably in his early thirties. One night she came in from a date with him and told us about a conversation they had just had. The man had described what it was like to have sex with a woman and be able to spend the night together. In those days we were all supposed to be virgins and no matter how physically involved we became with our boyfriends, most of us had never had sexual intercourse nor slept all night with a man. He had said that the best part about sexual intercourse for him was afterwards when the woman was lying peacefully in his arms with her breasts against his chest. He had told my friend that as wonderful as it felt to be aroused and fully engaged sexually, that this calm and close time was the best physical feeling he knew.

I listened to her with longing and imagination, my heart pounding in my ears. One day I would share this closeness with a man and lie naked against his chest. One day I would know what that felt like.

Over the years I often thought of this conversation from late at night in the dorm. I found, too, that there was nothing more physically satisfying than to lie satiated in my lover's arms and feel that physical oneness and blending of skin surfaces that takes place after sex when all mounting tension has melted away.

To lose all feeling in my breasts and to no longer even have the simple and basic sensation of skin touching skin was devastating. There are so many simple pleasures that we take completely for granted until we lose them.

In spite of these lost sensations, I still felt desire as much as always and I still felt desirable.

There were over twenty-five of us in the room. We had come together to talk about life, not disease. We had come together to talk about living, not dying. We had come together to talk about dating, to talk about men, to talk about *sex*.

I had decided that I wanted to start a support group focused on dating and intimacy for single women who had been through mastectomy. I had been co-facilitating a family and friends support group for well over a year with another woman whose sister had also died of breast cancer. Listening to people tell their painful stories of their mothers, sisters, daughters and friends was rewarding. Those sessions had always brought me close to my sister. Afterwards, I would feel like I had just spent time with Jodie.

It was often quite difficult listening to all the horrors people were experiencing and I sometimes had great ambivalence about continuing my participation. It was gratifying to provide support for others but it was exceedingly painful to relive my sister's hell through them and to be reminded so vividly of my own connection to breast cancer. There was surely the satisfaction from the good I was doing and the dedication to Jodie. I liked giving my time to honor my sister and much preferred it to donating money to a cause without actually giving anything of myself, but this total immersion in breast cancer often felt suffocating. I wanted to stop living in chemotherapy, hair loss, suffering, and worrying about what to say to a mother, sister, daughter or friend, who was diagnosed with or dying of breast cancer. ***I wanted to focus on life.***

The outcome of my struggle was a "Dating and Intimacy After Mastectomy" support group. Throughout my breast loss and reconstruction period, I had had a loving companion and sexual partner who had been with me in the sweetest and most wonderful way. I had finally ventured out from this dear, safe but incomplete relationship into the brave new world of scarred and breastless intimacy. I wanted to share my new risks and rewards with others and I wanted to learn how they were experiencing their own adventures. I also wanted to help pave the way for those who hadn't stepped out yet.

The diversity of the group that came together in response to the posting for "Dating and Intimacy After Mastectomy" was astounding. There were women there of all ages, sizes, appearances, backgrounds and experiences. We were all quite excited to be there, but also somewhat tentative. None of us knew what to expect.

One woman told of having her breast removed at age twenty-nine. She, like so many others, had had zero family history of breast cancer and had always thought that breast cancer happened to older women only. She was strong and defiant in her decision to go forward without breast reconstruction. She knew about warrior women from ancient civilizations who gave up one breast to be able to hunt and kill more successfully with bow and arrow.

Someone showed us her prosthesis and said how hot, bulky and uncomfortable it could be. She shared her journal with the group and read to us what she had proudly and emotionally written about her remaining breast.

Another had joined a dating service and told of the resulting fiascoes. She described how difficult it had been to tell a man, she was dating and liked a lot, about her single-breasted state. She told of one lover who had left her because he couldn't deal with her half-filled chest. She spoke of an older man with whom she had shared outdoor camping adventures and eventually sex, but with whom she would not want to share emotional intimacy and life partnering.

There was a woman in her mid fifties who described her latest boyfriend and how unsatisfying their love-making was. It was clear that the dissatisfaction came from the barriers this man had to intimacy and had nothing to do with his reactions to the woman's breast reconstruction and faded scars. She had such a distinctly "I can handle anything!" style and tone.

There was another quite young, vibrant and strikingly beautiful woman who had just had her mastectomy surgery and was obviously devastated to be going through the assault of breast cancer in the prime of her youthful sexuality and mate searching. She had ended a fairly new relationship when she found out she had breast cancer. She did not want to know if the man could handle it; she didn't want to deal with rejection or have to focus on his problems and concerns about breast cancer. More importantly she needed one hundred percent of her attention on making her body whole again and needed to clear her life of distractions. It was obvious how sensual and sexual she had always been. She did not seem at all victimized by her breast cancer diagnosis, but rather had simply taken charge of her life. She was definitely okay on her own, and even preferred to be uncoupled, during this timeframe. You could taste her desire and passion as she spoke, and knew from listening to her that she would go back "out there" more beautiful and desirable than ever.

One woman described going through menopause as a result of chemotherapy. She had not yet had children and wanted to. She was tearful as she described all of the decisions she was facing. They had taken healthy eggs from her ovaries prior to chemotherapy and she had a young aunt who was willing to be a surrogate mother for her baby. Unquestionably her sex life had been greatly affected by all of this - on both emotional as well as physical levels.

I told the others about my venturing out finally from the seven-year relationship I had and risking intimacy with a new man with whom I had fallen deeply in love. I described how sad it had been to feel his hairy chest with my hands but to feel nothing of that warm softness with my breasts. I shared with the group what I had just written the night before:

Tears
April 25, 1995

When my sister died, I threw dirt on her casket as it was lowered into her grave and said, "I love you, Jodie.", sobbing bitterly. Three months later when I was diagnosed with breast cancer, I never shed a tear. For the next two years, I kept myself protected in a cocoon and never once cried freely or fully. The tears would arrive but wouldn't flow.

And then I met a man and knew immediately that this was the right man to whom I could expose not only my reconstructed body but every corner of my soul as well. I came out of my cocoon and spread my wings.

Now, he has pulled back; he will not go to the next level with me. Now, the tears pour forth.
-I cry because I will not have him.
-I cry because he will not let this be.
-I cry because he is withholding.
-I cry because he sees limitations that do not exist.
-I cry because he cannot give.
-I cry because I have risked and lost SO MUCH.
-I cry because I have been so strong and *not cried*.
-I cry because such a rare and deep connection is being severed.
-I cry because of loss.
-I cry because it is time to cry.
-I cry because *I can* again.

For days these tears have flowed freely without need for control. They have been there on the street when I am alone – walking, thinking. They have been there when I share my pain with friends and loved ones. They have been there to reflect the depth of my feelings.

I do not thank him for the pain, but I thank him for the tears.

And as we went around the room and shared our stories, it became apparent that some of us were highly open and out there in our sexuality and sensuality and others were rather repressed, private and not as free with our bodies. We were almost naturally divided into two camps. Those of us in the "free" camp began energetically and humorously to call ourselves "The Sluts". I was reminded of a card that my friend, Rita, had sent me for my birthday: "Good girls go to heaven." And then inside: "Bad girls go everywhere!" It became so clear that who we all were sexually, prior to breast cancer, was still who we were after breast cancer. It was also evident that a diagnosis of breast cancer can leave some people totally victimized or just the opposite can occur: it can turn one's perspective of life one hundred and eighty degrees in the other direction.

It was an exhilarating evening for everyone. We laughed. We cried. We exposed ourselves. We described our fears, our sadness, our anger and our anticipation of what was to come. By the end of the meeting many of us had actually opened our blouses or lowered our necklines to reveal to each other what our reconstructed breasts or breastlessness actually looked like. The sisterhood that immerged that night nourished us all; it became palpable to us and we left there with more than we could ever have anticipated when we first arrived.

In my family, women nurse their babies, no generation skipping, no exceptions. Among my major life passages and key experiences, nursing my son stands out from all others for its endearing sweetness and calming satisfaction. It was such a basic and natural way of expressing love and providing sustenance, a tender act, pure, primitive and completely physical.

J. was born six weeks early and soon became jaundiced as his tiny liver tried unsuccessfully to be fully functional. Until his fragile body stabilized, he was kept in an incubator under ultra violet light with his eyes covered to protect them from UV exposure. Seeing my new and naked baby hooked up like a laboratory experiment, confined inside that little aquarium-like box was emotionally overwhelming. I was informed that when infants had this condition, which was quite common among premature babies, their systems were unable to tolerate breast milk. The pediatrician was completely unaware of and unconcerned about the impact of his words when he told me, "So you won't be able to nurse him; what's the big deal? He's going to be just fine in a week or so. That's all that matters."

I felt heartbroken. Nursing my baby was critically important to me. Fortunately, within hours after hearing this upsetting news, my obstetrician informed me that I would be able to express the milk from my breasts while my baby was being treated and that as soon as his blood counts returned to normal, I would be able to begin nursing him again.

Leaving the hospital without him was terribly painful. At home I continued using the breast pump as I had been instructed. After only a few days, which seemed like an eternity, I finally brought my precious, healthy son home with me to hold in my arms and nurse.

During those early days, in spite of warnings not to, I refrained from ever using a bottle to feed J. Many people had told me that babies had to work much harder to get milk from their mothers' breasts than required with bottle-feeding. I wanted a guarantee that my baby would never reject my breast for a rubber nipple. Just as I had been cautioned, he became totally conditioned to breast feeding and would not accept nourishment from any other source. I turned my infant into a breast "junkie" and became captive in a prison that I, myself, had totally created; I could go nowhere without my baby for more than about two hours at a time. And no one else could feed him but me. It was a precious confinement that, over time and with much coaxing, slowly and eventually became balanced with bottle feedings and longer periods of freedom from nursing.

One night when J. was ten months old, *he* weaned *me* from nursing. He was gentle yet firm about it. We were on a Caribbean cruise and by then I was nursing him only once a day, before I put him down to sleep each night. It was a sweet private time alone together with night-night singing and peaceful rocking. Basically J. no longer needed to nurse; the nightly breast feeding before bedtime was more for my benefit than for his. It was as if he sensed the need for weaning me, when he took his small hand, after a few moments of nursing, and firmly and resolutely pushed himself away from my breast. That was the first and only time he had ever done that. He never once wanted or tried to nurse again.

As time passed, I would get a flood of memory and sensation related to nursing J. The exact feeling of milk traveling down to and swelling the nipples would explode in my breasts. It was quite striking to sense that so strongly when no milk was there.

Now, years later, with no "connected" nipples and zero sexual arousal obtainable through my reconstructed breasts, I can still feel the exact physical sensation of milk rushing into my nipples, whenever I want to recapture what that sweet experience felt like. It totally baffles me how this can happen. Since there's no "here" here, since all the nerve endings in my breasts were removed or severed, since my imitation nipples were made from non-breast tissue and are totally numb, how can I still have this strong physical response which took place in my body twenty-four years ago? And what makes it so easily available to experience the sensation of nursing, almost "on command", when there is no access at all to sexual stimulation through my nipples?

Sometimes it just takes faith and acceptance. It is good to sense that, even breastless, I will be able to feel for the rest of my life, both emotionally and physically, the joy and contentment of nursing tenderness.

Cynthia Leeds Friedlander
Sweetest Son and Friend

We lived on Paradise, Island in the Bahamas from the time my
son, J., was eighteen months old until just before his third
birthday. J.'s father had come home one night from work in New
York City and asked me how I would like to live in Nassau for
three to six months while he set up an offshore bank for his
employer. My memory would always distinctly ensure me that I
had immediately left the dinner table, walked upstairs to our
bedroom and begun packing as soon as those words left his mouth.
Certainly, in reality, a slightly different chain of events must have
taken place, but clearly I had zero hesitancy in my desire to go live
in Nassau with my husband and baby.

There was a wonderful freedom living there that contributed
tremendously to my son's development and sense of self. We
owned no possessions except for our clothing. I never needed to
say no to my son and I never had to keep him from touching
objects because they were dirty or dangerous. We bathed
regularly there but it seemed hardly necessary. Everything was
clean and we were in that crystal clear Caribbean water every day.
Paradise Beach was J.'s park and playground. He missed two
winter's of snowsuits and I read at least three novels a week,
collected seashells endlessly and developed quite a competitive
tennis game.

The Bahamian people were proud, gentle and extremely respectful
of each other. Living next to New Providence Island was
educational in basic interpersonal ways. We learned simple
courtesy that for the most part was foreign to New York City and
seemed to be disappearing throughout "civilized" cultures. In
Nassau, no Bahamian would pass another Bahamian on the street
without greeting the other. I watched as tourists would ask for
towels on the beach or directions to go somewhere, without asking
first, "Good morning, Sir. How are you today?" and then wonder
why the responses they received from the Bahamians were often
so rude. We also gained rich patience and deep relaxation living
in Nassau that I vowed to bring back to New York with me and
which I would always hunger for when I left.

At some point while we were living in Nassau, J. asked me where babies came from and I answered his questions simply and honestly. He also "smoked" his first and only cigarette ever there. We were at his father's office and someone had left a cigarette burning in an ashtray. J. asked me what it was and how people did it. I told him he could try it if he wanted, giving him no warning about how it might be. He breathed in heavily from that cigarette and choked for five minutes afterwards with tears burning down his face. He never ever wanted to smoke again after that, even into high school, college and adulthood.

One night at dusk just before we left Nassau I walked down the beach with my dear friend, Len, who was also my tennis pro. J. was running naked along the water's edge. Len's chocolate skin and my baby's golden sun-browned naked body on that pale sandy beach against that deep turquoise water were so strikingly beautiful. The magnificence of those images would inspire me to come back to New York and attempt to turn my home into all of those luscious colors, so that I could hold on to that state of calm and splendor. We returned home by cruise ship and J. would ask me as we walked off of the boat back into the contrasting harshness of New York City, "Mommy, why is the water yellow?"

When J. was four years old, we were waiting at the airport to go to visit my parents in Florida. I asked him in a quite conversational tone, "J., you know Daddy wants us to have another baby so much and I'm not sure if I want to do that. How about you? Would you like to have a baby brother or sister?" He looked at me squarely in the eyes and quickly responded, "Well, you know, Mom, it's not up to me. It really doesn't matter if I want a baby brother or sister. You can't have a baby if you don't want one."

Later when J. was in kindergarten, he walked up to me in the kitchen one night and out of nowhere said, "I like you; I love you. It never started and it never stops."

Where did this child, with so much wisdom and sensitivity beyond his years, come from? It was wonderful to be always able to talk to him easily about any topic and know that he could and would take it all in and make it his own.

When his father and I separated and later divorced, it was painful for all three of us. Broken homes and split families had no appeal. All in all, we managed as well as we could and J. grew in ways that I wished he had not been compelled to but in ways that made him even stronger and wiser than he already was.

When my sister was dying of breast cancer and my son had just graduated from high school, I had a long talk with him about his fear of my life ending as his Aunt Jodie's was. I told him how often I had mammograms and promised him that if I did get breast cancer that it would be dramatically different from how my sister's story had unfolded and that he did not need to be afraid of my dying of breast cancer.

Jodie died the day J. was supposed to leave for his freshman year of college and I encouraged him to go to Boston as planned rather than travel to his aunt's funeral in Virginia. I wanted him to have a normal and wonderful new beginning and I knew that my sister would have wanted that for him too.

The following December, I waited until after J. had finished his exams and until he arrived in Florida for Christmas vacation, to tell him that I had been diagnosed with breast cancer. I had decided not to tell my parents about my diagnosis but I needed to tell J. We always spent that time of year with my parents in Florida and it was going to be extremely demanding for me to spend those ten days there with carcinoma in situ inside my body and with no words about that coming from my mouth the entire visit. I needed J.'s strength and support to lean on during that time.

My father and I drove to Fort Lauderdale Airport to pick J. up from his flight from Boston. I told my father that I wanted to drive home via Route A1A so that J. and I could walk on the beach together. It was easy to tell J. about my breast cancer, knowing that there was no threat to my life and knowing I could count on him to be my cushion and confidant during those challenging days in Florida.

In February, when I had my bilateral mastectomy and breast reconstruction surgery, J. came home from college to be there with me. He was there at my side just before I went into the operating room. I had already been prepped for surgery and had an I.V. needle in my hand. The plastic surgeon, Jim, came by to see me before the anesthesiologist put me under and rolled me away for mastectomy. Jim needed to draw on my chest so that he would have guidelines to follow after the breast oncologist had completed the first part of that two-part surgery. When Jim walked up and began to open my gown to make his marks, J. shouted out, "Stop, that's my Mom!" Jim had thought that J. was my boyfriend. That episode provided much-needed comic relief in a most pressured time. The look of horror on J.'s face was quite amusing and I always loved it whenever people thought we were so close in age. I would certainly have given up my amusement and satisfaction to spare J. this brief terrifying moment if I had suspected in any way what was coming when Jim arrived.

J. would bring his girlfriend and two of his friends from college to watch "The Crying Game" on video in my hospital room two nights later. I thought how cool it was that I could be so "unsick" after such serious surgery and that my son was comfortable enough with my situation to bring new friends of his, whom I didn't even know, to visit me in the hospital.

Having J. as my son provides great richness to my life. We have always been close friends and confidants. We fish, ski and play tennis together. We both love words and use them always to our own advantage. We share an appreciation of and enthusiasm for life that is quite similar. I know I have tremendously influenced J.'s strong handle on the world and his ease with people and I know that I have learned more from him than anyone else. I treasure his wisdom and perspectives more than I can express.

I like him; I love him.

It never started and it never stops.

When I gave up my breasts, I developed a longing to own a dog again. From the time I was a young child, I had always adored dogs. My sister and I had shared this adoration and had passed it on to our own children. The two dogs that I had grown up with were definitely like siblings to me. They shared all of my secrets and provided pure and unconditional love, always and abundantly. Whenever I reflected on my childhood and tried to conjure up my happiest moments, most often there were images of playing with dogs. My sister had owned four dogs at the time of her diagnosis of breast cancer. I realized how significant having a dog was to me and knew that this would be the perfect gift to give myself to compensate for the loss of my breasts. Buying a dog would be a way to celebrate my life and to commemorate my sister's life as well.

My sister had raised many dogs and assisted in the whelping of several litters of puppies over the years. When she was diagnosed with breast cancer, she owned Sadie, a white West Highland terrier; Mandy, a sandy colored Llassa Apso; Amelia, a black and white Shitsu; and Charlie, a tiny Yorkshire terrier. Three of these dogs were dispersed to other homes because of Jodie's illness. Sadie went to the dogs' caretaker and family friend. Mandy went to Jodie's daughter, Leslie. And Amelia went to Jodie's son, Paul. Charlie, who was the only male dog my sister ever owned, stayed by her side and comforted her throughout her illness. When Jodie was finally hospitalized and would not be returning home again, we hid Charlie in a bag and took him to the hospital to visit her. In preparation for that special visit, I had spent hours brushing and untangling his long show quality hair and bathing him. Within a month after Jodie's death, Charlie, who was only four years old, mysteriously died of an unknown cause. I wanted to think that he needed to be with her or that she was granted her desire to have him by her side again.

Wanting another dog grew stronger and stronger as my year of breast surgery progressed. Everyone said to me, "What do you want to own a dog for? You have total freedom now that your son no longer lives at home. And you are never there anyway! Why would you want to tie yourself down with that kind of responsibility?" They were right. I had responsibility for no one other than myself. I was always running from my home that felt lonely to me. There was no husband and no child living there anymore. It was an empty place. I wanted a dog to have a reason to come home. I wanted to decrease my meaningless freedom. I wanted some responsibility that felt familial. I wanted a dog to fill the emptiness in my chest where my breasts had been, where my sister love had been.

"I've found my dog. She is a ten month old, two and a half pound Papillon named Puffin", I announced to my dear companion, Jake, after a telephone conversation with a breeder in Schenectady. "You can't buy the first available dog you locate! We'll need to do some research and see lots of puppies before you can buy a dog." So Jake, and I made three trips to look at Papillon puppies.

The Papillon, pronounced *"pah pee yohn",* is one of the oldest purebred toy dog breeds. The name, Papillon, which means butterfly in French, comes from the breed's fringed and always alertly up and spread ears that dramatically resemble the wings of a butterfly.

With each visit to research and find my chosen butterfly dog and "breast replacement", I began to have second thoughts about the breed. All the dogs we saw looked totally different from the ones I had seen previously in person, photographs, books and dog shows. They were also much bigger than the dog that I wanted.

Finally it was time to drive up to Lake George to see Puffin. When we walked into the breeder's summer home on the lake, this tiny, tiny beautiful dog came running/leaping down a long corridor to greet us. She was definitely gazelle-like in her movement. Her joyfulness, friendliness and curiosity were abundant. When I picked her up she kissed my face all over with her tail wagging incessantly. She was so small, although fully grown, that I could get my forefinger to touch my thumb when I wrapped the fingers of one hand around her waistline. This was exactly the little dog I wanted.

What a surprise that this tiny animal that I chose to fill the emptiness left in my chest after breast cancer, turned out to be not only the equivalent size of my missing breasts but so like me in style and temperament, it was almost scary:

> -She is independent to a fault. She loves being with others but absolutely thrives on her own.
> -Her hair is fringed around her face, flowing abundantly, wildly and freely in front of her ears.
> -There is a charm and elegance about her that commands attention.
> -She is warm and welcoming, comfortable with everyone and rarely intimidated.
> -She is endlessly entertaining.
> -She is always playful and has to be in the middle of everything that is going on around her.
> -She confidently believes she is loved by all and never is shy or timid.
> -The range of her vocal expressiveness is amazing.
> -She is exceedingly communicative and can easily convey all that she wants clearly.
> -She never withdraws but always lets you know what is wrong or if she has a need or desire.
> -She is adventurous and quite rugged, well beyond her size and appearance.
> -She always wants to play and has endless energy.
> -She takes her responsibility seriously of warning others of perceived danger and cannot be deterred from what she knows she must do.

I could have never imagined that this three-pound animal would replenish so abundantly the big void in my life. Bringing Puffin into my world completed the full circle I needed, after my sister's death and the loss of my breasts. Jake always said what a wonderful and invaluable investment Puffin was, "She pays dividends every day!"

Cynthia Leeds Friedlander

Influence and Identity

Cynthia Leeds Friedlander
Influence and Identity

My life has been colored by a vision of men. I have always worshipped my father. I was completely boy-crazy as a girl. Many of my key life choices were made in reference to males, until I finally got off of the pedestal after I had been married for nine years and was already a mother. My grown son is also one of my dearest friends whose perspectives and opinions I value and respect more than anyone I know.

When I was quite small I learned about war and how only men served in the military. I was glad I was a girl who would never have to be in the army and thought that war was horrendous. There could be no reason for people to kill each other. I did adore playing with my toy cap gun and wearing my leather holster with the fringe. The attraction to them was the apparel and accessory aspect of the holster, the exciting sound of the caps going off and especially their smell after firing. Even though we all dramatically pretended to be dying when we were "shot", I never thought about death or killing anyone when we played with guns.

We rode brooms for our horses and made loud whispering noises to represent the sound of galloping hooves: pteeco pteeco pteeco, with heavy accents on the consonant sounds. I was always a cowboy and not a cowgirl, when I played those make-believe games. We must have been shooting at Indians, although we also played that we were the Indians as often as we played we were the cowboys. And as an Indian, I again chose the male roles. My bow and arrows held as much appeal as my toy gun and holster. I made no distinctions about who were the good guys and who were the bad guys. We just needed enough parts and adventures to go around.

Sometimes it was rocket ships we were using for transportation and instead of brooms for horses we used the swing set for our space vessel. I always wanted to be the captain and once again that meant taking a male role in all of those pretend games. Unless I was playing school teacher or mother with my dolls, playtime was filled with male roles that I wanted to be.

Even though I was attracted to all of those male identities of influence and adventure, I was intensely feminine and definitely not a tomboy. I grew up in a time when there was a traditional image of the clear differentiation between the roles of men and women. My mother was not a conventional homemaker but rather shared a business with my father. She was a creative multi-talented businesswoman whom I admired tremendously. I loved the time I spent at home without either parent there and I loved the time I spent in the family store working side by side with my parents.

There was a series of women who worked for my parents in the home when I was growing up. They were all proud women, who wore uniforms, whom we called maids and who were in those days identified as colored. I loved those women as much as if they had been family members. I hated it that when I rode the bus to junior high school, none of the kids would sit next to those African American domestic cleaning women who rode the same buses on their way to work.

One day, one of them said to me in response to a remark I made about what I was going to be when I grew up, "Lawd, chile, you don't have to worry yo'self about what you're gonna be when you grow up. Some rich man is gonna take care of you." I never articulated my mixed feelings about her comment and I never forgot it. How wonderful and secure to be taken care of and have no worries. How awful to be taken care of, to be *trapped* by *ownership* and not provide for yourself. It wasn't until years later, after I had married and divorced the *perfect* husband, that I read a quote by Malcolm Forbes that rang so true to me and also articulated what I must have felt when she had made that comment long before. "There's nothing more expensive than a free lunch."

It is amusing yet somehow strange to see how I often made decisions relative to the allure and/or appearance of a man:

> -When I was in the eighth grade I auditioned for the ninth grade choir. *The music teacher was handsome and charming.* All of the kids were crazy about him. Being in the ninth

grade choir was part of being in the in-crowd. I couldn't sing. When I auditioned, he told me he was going to put me on the front row of the choir where he could look at me but I had to promise not to sing. *I adored him.*

-When I was in the tenth grade, there was a new teacher who taught drama classes and directed the drama club. *He was handsome and charming.* I signed up to be a line reader for plays and soon became heavily involved in all aspects of play production and performing. *I adored him.*

-When I was a sophomore in college, I changed my major to economics and business because my *handsome and charming* boyfriend was an economics major. I took one economics class and hated it. *The teacher was not handsome or charming. I did not adore him.* I found the subject matter boring.

So...

-When I was a junior, I changed my major once more to French. I had loved French in high school and had studied in France during the summer after my high school graduation. I had placed so high in my French language placement tests my freshman year of college that they had made me register for third level literature classes in which no French was spoken and the reading assignments were quite demanding. I had hated both classes and failed the second one because I never read any of the assignments or attended the classes. During the second semester of my sophomore year I had signed up for a French conversation class to practice speaking the language that I loved. *The professor was handsome and charming and very French. I adored him.* How else would one select a major?

A fire to make a difference in the world burned inside of me and a fierce spirit of independence drove me, while at the same time I always found ways to please my parents and keep from bringing them the kind of heartache my sister brought them. And I also dreamed of being in love and marrying my own Prince Charming. My sister had not married for two years after finishing junior college and until that marriage took place, my mother carried her eldest daughter's unmarried state with her like the ball and chain of a prisoner. And even when the wedding day came, there was so much displeasure for my mother, associated with the bridegroom and his family that I certainly didn't want my mother to go through that anguish with me. I would have to be married as soon as I finished college and my husband and his family would have to be all that my mother wanted for me.

Long after we had each become the mother of a single son and after each of our marriages had ended, I spent some wonderful time reminiscing with an old friend, Marilyn, that I had known since our infancies. As girls, giggling had always been the number one time expenditure for us and the years had changed nothing about our constant laughter. When we found and compared our old diaries, letters and scrapbooks from the fifth and sixth grades, we ended up in uncontrollable hysterical laughter. The contents of all of those wonderful mementos were comprised of nothing but boys, boys, boys! We had always talked about NJB's, as we referred to Nice Jewish Boys, when we were growing up, and both of us were sure that there weren't any in our town. Our lustful boy-drive was never stopped by that fact. Except for pretend boyfriends from pre-dating age, neither of us ever dated or had a Jewish boyfriend, until I found one in college and eventually married him.

My first true love, Ed, began in the summer after the eighth grade. My feelings for him were so intense that they frightened me. He was the first boy to touch my breasts but not the first boy I ever kissed. I often wondered how our lives would have proceeded if his family had not moved away the following summer.

Cam, my steady boyfriend, throughout high school, was my guardian and protector. He would defend my honor at all costs: No one could ever use the "F" word in front of me. Because he was not Jewish, my parents kept me from dating him when he went away to college. I protested their restriction but I was ready to move on and experience the world. He would always remain such a dear part of my past.

When I first met my future husband, Hank, in college, I didn't even like him particularly. He seemed slick and superficial. It wasn't until I met his family that I started to like him a lot. I actually fell in love with them as soon as I met them and even sent Hank a card right after I met his family that said on the front, "My mother warned me about boys like you!" and on the inside, "Gosh, I thought I'd never find one!"

As a French major, I wanted to go to France to study during my senior year of college. I was also quite motivated to go there so that I could spend time with my dearest friend, Billy, who was studying in Paris. We had become inseparable the summer after I graduated from high school when I went to France for the first time. Neither of us had ever been on an airplane and both were terrified to fly but thrilled to be going to France. He was my playmate and confidant and I was never happier than when we were together. There was a song whose lyrics described exactly how I felt about him, "Sunshine, lollipops and rainbows, everything that's wonderful, that's how I feel when we're together". He was the best dancer I had ever danced with. One night when I was home from college in the Star City, and we were out dancing, he made me promise him I would not marry my college boyfriend just because he was Jewish. So I went off to France to try to pick which man to marry: Mr. Right or Mr. Fun!

When I got to France, my playmate was there to meet me. He swept me off my feet with the biggest hug. Yet, I knew instantly that he was no longer there for me the way he had been in the past. He had met someone in France whom he was in love with and he was "*gone*". It was January of my senior year and I was graduating from college in the spring. I was terrified at the thought of being an *adult* on my own, rather than a student, supported by my parents. I was totally unprepared to be providing for myself. And for my mother's sake, it was time to be married to the right man who would provide for me and take care of me.

So, in April of that year I married Mr. Right who flew from New York to France for my spring break and took me to Italy where we were married in Rome in a civil ceremony. As terrified as I was of being on my own and providing for myself, I was equally as frightened of being married. On my wedding day, with no friends or family present, dressed in a beautiful French white silk crepe mini-dress with cloth covered buttons all the way down the front, I could not stop thinking, "What if we can never be divorced because we are getting married in Rome?" I knew there was no divorce in Italy but did not make a connection between that restriction and the Catholic Church. In spite of that fear, I had asked my husband-to-be to bring me a simple narrow gold wedding band to be married in. It was my intention never to remove that ring for the rest of my life.

After a honeymoon on the French Riviera, we came home to New York and in May were married again in Virginia by a rabbi with our families present.

My professors in France had let me return to New York with my husband, with the understanding that I could complete my semester's work back in the States by writing papers for each class. There had been no deadlines given to me for the completion of those papers. All I needed to do to graduate was to write them. Procrastination became a total way of life. I was disoriented as a new bride and I passed entire days, watching soap operas.

I spent the next year crying myself to sleep almost every night because
  -I missed my lost playmate, Billy.
  -I felt like I would never graduate because of those papers
    that I couldn't get myself to write.
  -I had given up my freedom.
  -I did not have work to do.

Cynthia Leeds Friedlander

-I was living next to the Long Island Expressway in Rego Park, Queens in a one-room apartment, overlooking the Expressway and a vast parking lot.

When my husband saw how miserable I was, he asked me if I wanted to end our marriage. I told him that I didn't want a divorce because it would be too humiliating but that if I could erase our marriage so that it had never happened, I would.

My grandfather died that year and my husband and I attended his funeral in Virginia. I thought ironically to myself, "Here lies the main reason you married a Jewish man." My grandfather was from the "old country" and would never have accepted my marrying a non-Jewish man. I suddenly saw the rest of my life in front of me, living a choice I had made to please my family rather than myself. It was the same kind of feeling I had on my wedding day in Rome.

When I was finally able to get myself to complete the papers so that I could graduate and get a job, I became happier. The next year, when we moved from Queens and I started teaching French, I fell in love with my work, with my husband and with married life. I never looked at another man, nor longed for my lost playmate, although I would dream of him for years. My husband and I traveled a lot, saw many movies every week and spent lots of time with our families. I was quite content.

After five years of marriage, we took a trip to Israel where my husband had been born. I returned from that trip filled with a sense of heritage and roots and was finally inspired to start the family that my husband so desperately wanted.

Within two months after that trip I became pregnant. When my son was born, I was ecstatic and decided not to return to work. Instead I wanted to become a full-time mother. Those were the happiest times and I always imagined having another child and staying married to the same man for the rest of my life. I was blissfully pleased with my existence.

When my son was eighteen months old, we moved temporarily to the Bahamas for my husband to set up an offshore bank for his employer. Our life was a paradise there. One day, I was in the swimming pool with my toddler and another young mother and her baby. She was describing to me how inattentive her husband was, how unhelpful he was with their baby and how he had not even been there with her in the Labor Room when her baby was born. I was describing my perfect little life. My husband had certainly been there every minute with me in the Delivery Room. He had walked the floors many nights with our crying baby even though he had to be at work the next day and I did not. He was the best husband and father in the world. The blond woman looked at me with her big blue eyes and said, "Oh, Cindy, you're *sooo* lucky." And I *was.* I knew how perfect my life was and I cherished it with all of my heart. My life revolved around my husband and my baby.

It was in Nassau that I became a voracious reader and so became inspired to write. My dependence on my husband for my identity and for my support was reflected in my early writing from that time:

Irony Revealed
Nassau, Bahamas
Fall, 1976

Last night I dreamed about Billy again. The same dream but new. This time I told him, "I love you." and did not want nor need an answer. I awoke and sensed the difference in my dream and lay awake thinking, rethinking and finally knowing.

But often, lucid nocturnal visions fade by morning. That sense of knowing remains; yet the knowledge lies hidden somewhere in dawn's shadows...

Okay, gutless wonder! Big talker, lots of words, lots of opinions. Is it all empty rhetoric? Why should writing be so much harder? Is it simply because I have less practice at it or is it that nothing I say or think is worth committing to paper – to permanence?

Stare at the blank page long enough and something worthwhile will come to mind. Certainly today has been out of the ordinary. Poor Elaine! (Poor me. Gutless wonder!) Honesty: the false front for cowardice:

It all began with those two black hands coming over the gate. "Who's there? What do you want?" I shouted. Muffled responses. I asked again.

Elaine was already under the bed when I finally understood, "Immigration." "I can't come out right now.", I said, slamming and locking the doors and pulling the curtains. Now what do I do? Poor Elaine, under the bed telling me to tell them that I was "fearful for the child and that the dayworker is not here today." Gutless wonder responds, "I can't lie to them, Elaine. My husband and I could be sent to jail too, you know. They must know you're here. You can't hide under the bed this way."

The final cop-out, of course, is calling Hank to come home, *please, now.* I venture into the yard again. "Madam why were you so rude before?" "I'm afraid of strangers." (meekly) "But we identified ourselves. You were so rude." "I didn't mean to be rude. Will you please wait here until my husband gets home?" (pleading)

I go back into the house and simultaneously try to appease and to ignore J. He is beginning to get suspicious. Children do have this sixth sense when trouble is in the air. Elaine remains under the bed imploring me to go out and tell them that no one is here. Of course I can't hear Elaine because J. is in high gear already. "Oh God, why isn't Hank home yet?" The minutes drip by like honey down the side of a jar – slow, sticky.

And he arrived and calmly handled all and poor Elaine was taken off to jail for being a Jamaican, for washing toilets, ironing shirts, loving a small boy, and on various occasions being surly, defiant and proud, while performing these and many other household duties and delights. But then, this is Nassau and there must be ten Bahamians unemployed for each one holding down a job, which may not even exist tomorrow. And

so Jamaicans are not welcome here. And so Elaine
will be sent away.

> *Hank: the center of my life.*
> *My rock: sensible, calm, responsible, reliable.*
> *My friend: funny, wise, loyal, fair.*
> *My lover: tender, passionate, gentle, unselfish.*
> *Hank: my life*

Thus is irony revealed. I write in search of self. I seek
independence and direction. Maybe I even seek a
merry-go-round's grab at that golden ring, Immortality.
And, yes, I even write to proclaim the strength and
glory of womanhood. How strange then, to begin with
a dream of lost youth's faded love, an afternoon of
weakness and inaction and an open admission of total
devotion to and dependence on one man.

So how did I get from that life to divorce? There were many steps
that created the irreparable chasm that grew between my husband
and me. I know I contributed to it greatly and I know he did as well.
"Latent adolescence" is the simplest all-purpose label I would often
use to describe why my marriage ended. I know what happened. I
know what choices I made. I know what choices he made. And I
know that for seventeen years I have lived apart from that man who
was the center of my life.

When I look back, I see my divorce as sad, painful, damaging and
wrong. I also see it as the biggest gift of my life:
  -I have gained so much from that loss. Breast Cancer is the
   only bigger teacher in my life.
  -I have become self-sufficient and independent which I have
   always wanted to be.
  -I have experienced many different types of relationships
   with many people I would have never known and loved if I
   had stayed married.
  -I have taken risks, tackled activities and become passionate
   about them, that I would have been too afraid of and never
   tried, as a "kept" and married woman.

-I have learned what kind of man I would most like to share
   my life with and I have endangered my heart many times
   looking for him.
-I have finally rid myself of neediness and am whole.

I went to an astrologist and psychic only one time in my life. She
insisted on knowing the exact hour of my birth. I went to see her in
a time of deep emotional pain. She knew about my inner being and
astounded me with information about my life and my way of existing
in the world. I wanted to know about love. I wanted to know if I
would have a life partner again. She said to me, "I see men in your
life." I answered her angrily, "I don't want to have men in my life. I
want to be married again. Aren't I ever going to be married again?"
She answered, "Can't you feel it? Don't you know that's what you're
working towards?"

And yes, she was right; there have been men in my life - some have
been friends and some have been lovers and they have all helped me
learn and grow:
   -There was Blair who first broke my heart and taught me the
      painful lesson that I could be left by a man who was deeply
      in love with me.
   -There was loyal, faithful Jake, my fishing guide and
      bodyguard, who stayed by my side for seven years that
      included my sister's battle with breast cancer and my own.
   -There was Patrick, a physician, who briefly passed through
      my life to help me say good bye to my breasts when I was
      diagnosed with breast cancer.
   -There was my dear friend, Edward, who helped me regain
      confidence about my newly reconstructed breasts.
   -There was Howard, the man of my dreams, the man I
      wanted to spend my life with, the man I gave up Jake for …
      the man who left me because he wanted to find a younger
      woman to have babies with.
   -There was Ned, the man of extremes, who brought me so
      much laughter that I finally stopped hurting from losing
      Howard.

- There was Jusef who came from an extremely different culture from my own, who showered me with affection and who, I knew, would not, could not be the life partner that I sought.
- There was David, the widower I adored, who fled from me when I lost my job.
- There was Dan, my young playmate, who ran and hiked with me and gave me respite from heartache.
- There was Jesse who brought out in me a deep and primitive passion that I would never, before or after, know anything sweeter or surer.

And so, after all these years, after all these men, after all these losses, I know what I want:

- I want a life partner, a friend, a playmate. I want fidelity from him and for him.
- I want to give with no demands.
- I want equality, *mutuality,* trust and respect.
- I want to share the good, the bad, the everyday.
- I want passion, intensity, electricity.
- I want calm and quiet with no need to talk at all.
- I want to talk and connect through words. I want to bare my soul without fear of judgment or rejection.
- I want my privacy, independence, and self-sufficiency and--
- I want to give that to my partner – for him as well.

Having breast cancer and going through bilateral mastectomy and breast reconstruction surgeries initially seemed like huge deterrents to finding a mate, to coupling and to sexual intimacy. It was quite scary in the beginning to be *out there* without natural breasts - the very body parts that seem most to define a woman's sexuality. It is gratifying to know that I feel strengthened and even enhanced, both physically and spiritually, as a result of my encounter with breast cancer. It is actually quite wonderful to learn from experience that there are men who do not recoil from women who have had breast cancer, who have lost the sexual functioning of their breasts, who are deeply scarred.

It is good to have the perspectives that I have to share with other women and men who are dealing with any type of scars, disease or dysfunction and their effects on intimacy and sexuality.

Men and Breasts: Remembrances

Time of Innocence

It was a time of innocence. My first kiss had been when I was fourteen - late for a first kiss. He had been a short basketball player, a grade ahead of me. He was taking me to my first formal school dance and I liked him a lot. He was my first "older" boyfriend and I knew I had to do this *finally*. I wanted to. For many nights before that dance, I had practiced kissing my pillow, wanting to be able to do it *right*, wanting to do it well.

I wore a pale blue chiffon strapless long dress, with my first pair of dyed-to-match shoes, to the dance and he brought a wrist corsage to the door when he came to get me. Later that night, at a friend's house, it happened.   It was a sweet and tender kiss and for the rest of my life I would always be able to recreate the exact sensations of his lips on mine.

There had been kissing games for years prior, spin-the-bottle and post office. I had never participated. One night after a party, my much older sister had laughed at me when I told her that I had left the room when the game had begun. I told her that I thought it was silly for twelve-year-olds to be kissing. We were too young to be doing that. And what was the point anyway? You ended up kissing someone you may not even like or want as a kissing partner. If I were going to kiss someone, it was going to be because I *wanted* to kiss *him* and not because some spinning bottle had ended up pointing at him. Even though I deeply felt the peer pressure that comes with those delicate years, I was strong enough in my own identity and self-awareness to follow my own head and heart.

A year after my first kiss with the basketball player, I found myself totally in love with a new boy in town, Eddie, and completely frantic that, at such a young age, I could have such deep feelings for a boy. This felt serious and it frightened me.

And just as that first kiss was burned forever in my memory, so was the intensity of those emotions for Ed. This was *first love*, tingling sweet and delicious, like the tiny pearl of nectar at the base of a honeysuckle blossom. And that taste of honeysuckle and the heat of a clear summer night would also become permanently engraved into remembrance:

Ed and I had been at The Center, a place where we all used to go to dance. That night I was sleeping at a girlfriend's, who lived a few blocks away. Ed and I walked alone together with our arms around each other's waists in the still night, brightly lit by the moon, taking shortcuts through people's backyards to get to my girlfriend's house. I was wearing jersey knit Bermuda shorts, the color of lilac blossoms, with a matching lilac and white checked short sleeved cotton blouse. Ed's deep voice and hairy legs added to his appeal to me because they made him seem older than the other boys our age. We stopped in one of those yards, surrounded by the intoxicating fragrances of summer flowers, and kissed for quite a while. And then Ed unbuttoned my blouse, slid his fingers beneath my bra and gently touched my breasts, right there in the moonlight under a sky full of stars.

Going where I had never been before brought sensation and excitement that would never be experienced in that way again. It was the first time I had wanted to let a boy touch me so intimately and it felt, immediately and simultaneously, wonderfully right and guilt-laden. I experienced how scary and unsure youth was, even though I was so sure of my feelings and myself.

Ed's family moved again the next year, and I felt the first pain of lost love. I knitted him a sweater, repeating a mantra with every knit two, pearl two: "I love you, Ed. Love me, Ed.", as if I could hold our love together and make it last forever through the very stitches I was interlocking with my knitting needles. For several months we wrote each other letters of undying love and to this day whenever I hear the song, "Take Good Care of My Baby", I feel all the bittersweet feelings from that time of Ed and innocence.

Longest Kiss and Deep Scars

Blair and I met through business. He had been referred to me as a speaker for my seminars. I had zero interest in a romantic involvement with him. My purpose in meeting him for lunch was to thank him for being such a good presenter and to build a strong professional alliance with him. I learned that day at lunch that he was a frustrated writer, read voraciously, and loved words and language as much as I did. I also learned that he had a stale marriage, an alcoholic wife and four children. He told me, "I've never had an affair before but I'd really like to. My marriage is so worn down." I laughed in his face and basically made fun of him a bit. "You can't go looking for that sort of thing. You can't just make it materialize like that. Something like that happens out of the blue when you least expect it. You can't make it happen just because you're looking for it."

We began meeting after work for drinks and he kept taking later and later trains to go home. I somehow didn't notice how many drinks he always had. I was totally infatuated with him and his incredible command of language. We would talk endlessly and I was mesmerized by his words. No man had ever talked with me like that and I had never shared so much about myself with a man.

One night we met in the bar of a hotel on Park Avenue just south of Grand Central Station. We were sitting on a banquette in front of a window. It was very dark and smoky. Suddenly in mid sentence, we started kissing. It was one of the longest kisses I'd ever had; it just went on and on - gentle, playful, inviting, sensuous. It was obvious that we both had been longing and longing to do this; it was as if we were making up for all the time we had spent together without ever kissing. After our lips parted, he rolled out this deep sexy laugh and said, "Oh how disappointing; you can't kiss." Our relationship progressed slowly and seductively after that night of the longest first kiss in history.

One day I phoned him at work and asked him if I was bothering him by calling so often and he answered, "There is no way for you to call me too often." So we met when we could and played when we could and talked when we could. It was passionate and mutual and delicious.

Being with Blair aroused my senses and I began to write like I had never written before. It was intense and I loved sharing written words with him – mine, his or others'. We would talk about books and read to each other. And I would write for him and he would reinforce my love of writing.

On Valentine's Day, we met for lunch at a charming little French bistro in my neighborhood. It was a bitter cold day and there was bright sunshine gleaming in through the windows. I had written him a poem that I brought with me as a Valentine gift. After we were seated, I handed him the poem:

Yes

will you come to me yes
into me yes
and fill me up yes
make splendid yes

will you show me love yes
evergreen yes
and tender me yes
gentleness yes

will you laughter me yes
merriment yes
and play with me yes
frolicking yes

will you challenge me yes
pierce my mind yes
and bring vision yes
path blazing yes

will you come to me yes
into me yes
and fill me up yes
make splendid yes

He told me with tears in his eyes how touched he was by my writing and how beautiful he thought my poem was. We talked about Molly's "yess" soliloquy in James Joyce's *Ulysses* and I told him I had not even read Joyce and had not known of this incredible piece of writing when I wrote the poem for him.

We ordered lunch and continued to talk and talk the way we always did. He seemed less animated than usual and I did not hear any of his wonderful laughter that day. At some point he finally said to me, "You know the answer is no, don't you?" My ears heard his words but my heart could not take in what he was telling me. I never swallowed another bite of my lunch after that comment. He talked about the pressures he was under: work, drinking, family, and so on. I walked out into that bright sunshine after lunch with a pain as real in my heart as if he had placed a dagger there.

A close friend later said to me, "It's like he took you to the most wonderful amusement park in the world, showed you all the beautiful rides and candy and left you there all alone, penniless, voraciously hungry and with no tickets for the rides." Months later I was at a resort eating dinner and engrossed in a conversation when from out of nowhere I heard his voice in my head saying, "Oh how disappointing; you can't kiss." I had to run from the table to hide my tears. I thought I would never get over the hurt I was constantly feeling.

Blair had said to me once when we were talking about divorce and how damaging it was to people - to families, "You are so magnificently untouched and unscarred. I don't want to see you scarred." I was never good at recognizing foreshadowing; it never occurred to me that he was going to be the one to provide that first deep and lasting scar on my heart.

Soon after he said no, with my heart still aching, I lay down on the couch in my living room one night, laid my right arm across my chest and found my hand resting on something hard in my left breast. I was terrified. I was leaving town for vacation the next morning and my wonderful gynecologist agreed to meet me at his office that night to examine me. He told me I had a fibroid tumor in my breast and that fibroids were always benign. He said that there was a miniscule possibility that they could mask something that wasn't benign in the breast and that he always recommended removing them. He said that this was nothing that needed to be done right away and that I should go and enjoy my vacation.

When the benign fibroid tumor was removed from my breast, it left a thick ugly scar. It seemed somehow right to learn how badly my skin would form scar tissue after surgery, even fine plastic surgery that should leave little or no scarring. That scar under my left armpit on the outer rim of my left breast would always belong to Blair. So I was left with the kind of emotional and physical scars that I had never had before.

Out of the loss of Blair, I wrote about my breasts:

Explosion

I have just awakened with that fullness in my breasts again. That fullness that I want to give to you. Once before, I told you about this same feeling and you recognized the superlative beauty of my gift.

This time I lay in half sleep in my bed and felt the explosion at my nipples. And this time my senses defined the difference from my usual monthly soreness and tenderness which beg not to be touched. The contrast is enormous; this swelling pleads to be held, to be sucked from me. It is identical to the delicious agony of being full of milk while separated from the sole provider of relief: the newborn's mouth.

And I remember my first experience of this pain, my infant's first days home, my first separation from him. We were out for dinner, both sets of in-laws present, a family ceremony: celebration, drinking, laughter. The connecting link between a new mother and her baby is so constantly heavy and I had let it slip from consciousness to an infinitesimal degree for the first time since giving birth. My father, outspoken crude comic, was giving his opinion of the background music and the popular vocalist's singing ability, "She sounds like she has her tits caught in the wringer of an old-fashioned washing machine."

Wounded, I felt the weight of the forgotten chain: the liquid in my breasts poured forth. We all laughed at the wetness covering the front of my blouse, the reflex evidence of my father's remark. A sweet embarrassment. A sweet recollection.

And now my fullness reaches out for you. And you refuse my gift...

From Blair, I learned that I was "leavable" which was an important and unknown lesson for me to gain. I also learned that scars are meaningful to have; they show that you've survived loss; they show that you've lived; they mark significant events. Blair was the first to teach me how easy it is for a man to give up someone he wants passionately and loves deeply. This I would learn again several more times, yet *never ever understand.* And most important of all, from Blair I also came to know that ...

All wounds, no matter how deep, eventually heal and holding on to pain doesn't serve well.

My Fishing Guide and Bodyguard

Jake and I met playing tennis. We were paired as doubles partners one night in late August at a tennis party. At the end of that evening, Jake and I found out that we both loved tennis, fishing, running, outdoor adventures and skiing. Jake called me the next week to ask me if I'd like to play singles with him on Friday morning before he left the City to go to his house in the country. He had said that whoever lost could treat for lunch.

Jake's physical appearance was unusual and quite unlike anyone I had ever been attracted to before. He had a mean rugged harshness to him that I liked but did not find sexually or romantically appealing. He was exactly the kind of man to be with in New York City, though. He had that "Don't you even think about messing with me! " look. Ironically, as it turned out, he was the gentlest soul I would ever know.

We met for tennis and split sets. Jake had invitingly challenged me to a bet but there was no loser to pay for lunch. That day Jake and I shared two conversations that contributed greatly to the beginnings of the deep feelings that I would develop for him:

He told me about his diverse and adventurous background that was quite intriguing but what most appealed to me was Jake's description of bonefishing in Central America. He explained in great detail what bonefishing was like and when he came to the part where the bonefish took the bait, his sound effects of the fishing line being rapidly pulled out by this powerful but comparatively small fish, were so vivid that I felt like I was right there beside him on the flats with a fish on my line. Somehow I was quite taken by that man who had little in common with any man I had ever dated.

We also shared with each other some of the emotional pain we had both been through as our marriages had ended and we had both become divorced. I told Jake how awful I had felt when I had recently learned in a public setting from an aunt of my former husband that he and his new wife were expecting a baby in three months. Everyone in that family, including my son, had known about that pregnancy and no one had told me. Jake said that I could call him any time, night or day, if something was bothering me and I just needed someone to talk to. "What a nice man!", I thought to myself.

And so I began meeting Jake for tennis and lunch on Fridays. In early September, we bumped into each other at The US Open tennis tournament and he joined my friend from out of town and me for dinner afterwards. She was the one who had taught me to fish and she and Jake spent hours talking about antique maps, antique furniture, fishing, fishing gear and gardening. It seemed that they had much more in common than he and I did. After he left to go home, I said to her, "It looks like you and Jake are soulmates." She answered, "Cindy, it's rather obvious to me that he's in love with you." I just didn't see it.

Jake and I began to go out together more and more often and one night he told me that he had fallen in love with me and wanted to do whatever it would take to earn my love for him in return.

Soon after I began to fall in love with Jake, he took me to his wonderful house in the country, which had once belonged to his mother who had lived in it for several years. When she had grown older and the severe weather in the mountains had become too much for her, she had sold the house to a family who had eventually destroyed, abandoned and discontinued payments on it. Jake had purchased the totally ruined house from his mother for one dollar and spent the previous three years before he met me pouring every extra cent, all of his spare time and tremendous amounts of sweat, toil and love into rebuilding and refurbishing that house. The only pleasure that Jake had allowed himself during those three years was to learn to ski at a nearby ski resort.

Meeting Jake when I did could not have been better timed to enjoy all of his labors to transform that ordinary wrecked house into a charming, rustic and romantic hide-away. That first visit was in the fall and the weather had turned rather raw that far north. We hiked through beautiful wooded and secluded landscapes with magnificent mountain vistas. He took me to a fine restaurant called The Rowland House where a darling waitress named Ann waited on us. The food was delicious and in particular there was apple butternut squash bisque on the menu which we ordered and both found to be sensually smooth and tastebud pleasing. Jake said. "This is the best soup I ever put in my mouth. If you could make me soup like this, I would marry you."

The following week, I called The Rowland House and spoke to the chef who gave me the recipe for the apple butternut squash bisque. He said that he never gave recipes away but that my story was quite compelling and he wanted to provide me with the required love potion that I had pleaded for. Jake drove up to the country that Friday to winterize the house and finish planting his bulbs. He was planning to be back in the city for dinner at my house the next night. Around four o'clock in the afternoon on Saturday, he called to tell me that his car had broken down on the way back to the City and he didn't know if he could get back that night. I had spent hours preparing fresh chicken stock and cutting through the tough outside skin of several butternut squash. I said to Jake, "How frustrating for you to be stuck up there! I have something kind of special planned for tonight and if there is any way possible for you to get here, it would mean the world to me." And he did manage to get back. And the soup was delicious. And he couldn't believe how I had obtained the recipe. … And Jake and I never did get married.

I recognized that Jake was the richest poor man I had ever known. He earned much less money than I did but his life was abundantly full. Jake was an extreme loner. He liked his own company better than anyone else's and coveted his time alone. There was something about Jake, no matter how dedicated, worshipful and loyal he was, that was detached.

There was always a big difference between Jake's and my physical affection and sexual frequency desires and needs. I came to accept those differences and would even appreciate them tremendously later as I went through breast cancer diagnosis, breast removal and related surgeries a few years down the road, when sex became such a low priority for me during the hurdles of breast cancer and surgery.

Within a few months after we started dating, Jake and I saw how different we were and discussed what we wanted to do about it. Neither of us wanted to end our relationship or change the ingredients we were sharing and so we decided to stay together as a couple. Our relationship would continue to grow and deepen but would also always have certain limitations to it. In the spring after we returned from a ski trip in Utah, my sister was diagnosed with breast cancer. During the next two and a half years, Jodie was the number one priority. Jake was constantly there when I needed him and was ever attentive and able to provide solace and escape from those harsh and totally demanding times.

One day shortly before Jodie went into a final coma, Jake drove to New Jersey with me to visit her in the hospital, knowing it would probably be the last time he would see her. She had liked him tremendously from the moment she had met him. It was ironic that their first meeting had taken place when Jodie unknowingly had already had breast cancer, in early March, about six months after Jake and I had been dating each other seriously.

We had driven to Jodie's hand therapy clinic in Chatam, New Jersey. Charlie, Jodie's Yorkshire terrier, greeted us at the door. He was always at the clinic as her mascot and therapy dog. He had actually added therapeutic value for Jodie's patients, particularly children who were frightened of treatment. Jake had been having some severe wrist pain and Jodie provided him with therapy while we were there. Jodie had said how fatigued she had been feeling recently and also complained about pain in her left arm and armpit which she thought was caused by straining her arm trying to open a window in her clinic that had become weathered closed over the winter. Jake opened the window for her and repaired the damage so that the window would open and close more easily. Little did we know that the pain in Jodie's arm and her severe fatigue were both from advancing breast cancer.

More than two years later, on Jake's last visit to see Jodie in the hospital, we had a serious and loving conversation in the car during the drive. We talked about how deeply we felt for each other and how extremely different we were and our goals were. He said that he never wanted to live together or be married and he knew that I wanted a more shared and partnered life. When we arrived at the hospital we were both crying and stood on the sidewalk hugging each other. "Promise me you will always be my friend." I asked. "I will be.", he promised. We still never had said that we wanted to change or end our relationship.

When Jodie died, Jake drove me to Virginia for her funeral. Without Jake, I would never have been able to cope with all of those hardships that my family and I went through. Jake felt like family to me; I adored him and I could not imagine what my life would be like without him.

When I received a diagnosis of breast cancer exactly three months after my sister's death, Jake was there for me in ways I could never have expected from anyone. I would never be able to express all of my appreciation and adoration of Jake for all that he did for me. Throughout that entire next year, he was loving, patient, funny, supportive, kind, resourceful, understanding, loyal and more. He was always there when I needed him. He always made me feel wanted and desirable. He cooked, cleaned, fixed whatever wasn't working and he kept my life filled with beautiful flowers. When I was able, he took me fishing, skiing and played tennis with me. He was simply wonderful.

Shortly after my mammography appointment in which I was told that the mammogram indicated that I had carcinoma in situ and would need a biopsy done by a breast surgeon/oncologist, Jake went with me for an appointment with the second surgeon I was to see. That was the day in early December, 1992 when there was such a severe Nor'easter in New York City that the Hudson River and East River swelled over their banks and flooded both the East and West sides of Manhattan. The subways were so badly deluged with water that they stopped running and most buses were unable to follow their normal routes as well. Boats and feet were the only means of viable transportation that day in New York City, as Jake and I forced our way by foot for thirty-five blocks. The wind and rain were so harsh that it took over an hour and a half to get there. We had kept pressing our way uptown. When we finally arrived at our destination and entered the surgeon's office, there was a fussy lady who asked us to take off our boots to protect the already soaked carpet. I refused to accommodate her, saying that I had no desire to walk around in that office and get my socks and feet soaking wet. What a strange greeting after that long struggle to get there on a day like that! We were quickly distracted when a lovely medical receptionist came out to take our coats and make us comfortable after our horrendous journey. It suddenly seemed like we must certainly be where we belonged; it was Ann, our waitress from The Rowland House from years ago. The three of us recognized each other immediately although we had seen her only once again after that first night of butternut squash soup. It felt like we had come home and that this was where we belonged.

The appointment with the doctor felt the same. He was endlessly informative and kind. Jake and I left his office knowing he was the right doctor for my biopsy surgery and knowing that I would definitely be a breast cancer survivor unlike my sister.

At the end of January, before my surgery to remove both breasts, Jake took many nude photographs of me in his little country house so that I would always be able to remember what I had looked like. The sun was pouring in through the windows and I was surrounded by all of Jake's beautiful belongings that made that house so warm and personal. It felt right taking those photographs then as it would when we would take more later after my permanent implants were put in and my nipples were reconstructed.

When I had my breasts removed that February, I decided to pay for the super deluxe "Hollywood" accommodations that were available at the hospital. I had so many memories of misery from Jodie's hospital experiences. I did everything I could to make what I was doing as different from what she had been through as possible. The first day after my surgery, Jake looked at my newly reconstructed budding breasts with bandaged scars and drainage tubes and said the most perfect comment that any man could ever make to a woman who had just gone through bilateral mastectomy, "You're a babe!"

Jake stayed with me in my room after my surgery. When the phone rang he would answer it, "Beth Israel Racquet and Spa." The room was quite resort-like and hardly looked like hospital accommodations. There was a lovely sofa that opened up into a bed for an overnight guest. My second night in the hospital, I experienced a lot of pain and terrible reactions to the medications they had given me. I kept hallucinating horrible nightmarish visions and kept trying to wake up to escape from them. In my visions I was calling out for Jake who was just in the next bed from me but in actuality I was only dreaming and he couldn't hear me yelling out for help.

The following April for my mother's birthday, Jake went with me to Florida with my expanded, reconstructed breasts to tell my parents finally that I had been diagnosed with non life-threatening breast cancer in December and had ensured that I would never have another breast cancer diagnosis again by having both of my breasts removed in February. That communication was one of the most difficult ones I ever had to deliver. And there was Jake, ever by my side when I needed him.

I would spend seven years of my life with this wonderful and supremely devoted man. We drove to the country almost every weekend together. In the spring, summer and fall we fished and played tennis and in the winter we skied.

We bonefished in Belize and took ski trips to Maine, Utah and Wyoming. We made a spectacular trip to San Francisco, Yosemite and Mammoth Lake, where we ran, skied, played tennis and fished all in one incredible day but did not make love that night. It had been a nearly perfect day and I had wanted to get in all of my favorite activities in one day but Jake was too tired for the last one.

The many, many days we shared together in his darling country house were among the happiest times of my life. Fishing on Lake Londerbunk from Jake's canoe had to be the most fun I ever had and definitely the best respite I could find during those awful years of Jodie's horrible suffering.

I called Jake my fishing guide and bodyguard. I would always love him dearly – even after I ventured out to find a man who would want to share the deeper intimacy with me that I so desired and who would want to be my husband and life partner which Jake did not want to be. And even after, by doing so, I hurt Jake so badly that, he broke his only promise to me and could no longer be my friend as he had vowed he always would be, that tearful day in New Jersey in front of the hospital.

Last Touch

"We have to stop meeting like this." I enticingly said to the doctor examining my bare foot. It was the third attempt, after several years without success, to remove a wart permanently from the bottom of my foot. The dermatologist had told me the first time that eventually it would go away by itself anyway. It had come back each time it was removed and had interfered with sports activities that I enjoyed. It had also become quite painful. And so I had ended up back in Patrick's office to try again to rid myself of the annoyance.

On my first visit to his office, I had encountered Patrick as a happily married man with a family. A few years later I had learned that he was going through a divorce and we commiserated about the stress and strain of breaking up a family. I had always thought he was attractive but could get no affirmative response from him when I hinted about our seeing each other socially.

At that final visit to his office, I learned that he was closing his practice in New York and would be moving to Princeton, New Jersey in six months to begin a new practice there. That time, perhaps as a result of the fact that he would no longer be able to see me as a patient, he was more receptive to my flirting and asked me to go to dinner with him.

Our third dinner out together coincided with my having recently obtained my breast cancer biopsy report. It was bizarre telling someone I was just getting to know about my diagnosis of carcinoma in situ. It was also quite satisfying to be talking to a physician who could strongly reinforce my good fortune in having learned of my breast cancer at such an early stage. I had never liked taking advantage of a person's professional expertise in a social situation but I took full advantage of Patrick's medical knowledge and he seemed to understand my need to ask specific questions and talk about my upcoming mastectomy surgery.

Patrick would be the last new man that I would date while still possessing my natural breasts. We both knew that and we both were careful how we dealt with those circumstances. Patrick also knew that there was a man in my life whom I cherished dearly but with whom I would never move forward or marry. I certainly was interested in Patrick and definitely attracted to him. Under any other circumstances though, I would have never shared any intimacy with Patrick at that point in time. I knew that I wanted to feel a new man touch my nipples and caress my breasts one last time before they were taken from me and he knew it too. He was so careful not to hurt me since I still had healing wounds in each breast from the biopsy surgery.

I felt protected, exposing myself to him, because he was someone I had known for a long time, because I found him attractive, because he was a physician, which was greatly comforting to me, and because I needed that final experience before saying farewell to my breasts. There were tears in my eyes as he touched me and there were more tears when he told me that he would be there for me if I needed him. All I would have to do was call him. I truly appreciated his kind offer. I think he knew I would not call.

I saw Patrick only one more time after that night. He walked by, as my dear companion, Jake, was loading my car. We were going to drive to Maine for five days of skiing before my breast removal surgery. Patrick caught my eye as Jake had his back turned. He gave me a sweet wink and a small salute.

Within several more weeks he had moved his practice and was gone. I would never see Patrick again and the wart on the bottom of my foot never came back again.

Edward and I had first known each other through business. One day he called to ask me if I would go to the Philharmonic with him. I told him that I did not socialize with clients and he said, "Well, come with me to the Philharmonic and we can discuss that over dinner afterwards." He was charming and funny. I accepted.

As time passed, we became close. We always flirted with each other. Rather than become romantically involved, our relationship became one in which we shared our romantic entanglements with others. There was a strong attraction between us but we both recognized that there wasn't a true fit.

When my sister was diagnosed with metastatic breast cancer, Edward was there for me and for Jodie as well. He provided her with so much caring support that he was the one person she always wanted to talk to when she was at her lowest emotionally and most hopeless in her outlook.

When Jodie died and I wanted to pursue a malpractice suit against the internist who had put her on hormone replacement therapy, more than a year after her last mammogram, Edward was lovingly supportive but strongly discouraged my following that path. He described the grueling ordeal of that type of legal procedure, the huge emotional price I would pay and the insignificant satisfaction I would gain relative to the irreplaceable value of my sister's life.

When I found out I had breast cancer three months after my sister's death, Edward was one of the first friends I called. I knew I could always count on him for his generosity of heart and ever-ready sense of humor. I told Edward that I wanted to become an advocate for breast cancer. I said that I wanted to start an organization called *Vigilance* to educate women, particularly younger women, about the value of mammography, early detection and the fact that in such a large percentage of breast cancer patients there was no family history of breast cancer. Edward expressed his admiration for my quest and also warned me of the invasion of my privacy that this would produce. "You don't want your life to become totally focused on breast cancer! You want your life to be focused on living!"

One night when Edward was between relationships and my dear companion Jake was out of the country on a work assignment for a month, Edward and I went out to dinner together and ended up on my couch for a late night drink. It had been almost a year since my bilateral mastectomy and about three months since my nipple reconstruction. I certainly was not ready yet to venture out of my cocoon with implanted breasts but I did want to set the stage in some way.

Edward kept telling me that I was still as sexy as ever with my new breasts. I kept telling Edward how unnatural and unsexy I thought I looked with them. Finally we decided that I would show them to him in the flesh and he would feel them, to give me an impartial male reading. It was sweet and amusing. He had always been my biggest fan and that night was no different from before. "You're still hot." he kept repeating reassuringly and I just giggled. I was so grateful to a wonderful friend who paved the way for me to gain the confidence I needed to step out once again into the world of middle-aged dating which was crazy enough for the breasted and certainly beyond scary and intimidating for the breastless.

A few years later in early 1998, I took Edward to dinner on his birthday. He told me that he definitely wanted to be married by the end of 1998. I said that I wanted the same. We made a splendid agreement that if neither of us had found the person of our dreams by the end of the year, we would get married to each other.

In October of that year, I decided to end an electric and intense relationship that had begun in June. I had found the person that I wanted so much to be partnered with and I had been so sure of my feelings for him. I also clearly saw his resistance and need to pull away from the intensity that we shared together. Edward was amazed at how I, for the first time, had been able - after only four months - to let go of what I wanted most and had so much feeling invested in, because I deeply sensed the limitations that were there.

When I told Edward how devastated and hurt I felt and how hopeless it seemed to be once again out there uncoupled, he said to me, "Cind, you have nothing to worry about. You definitely have the best Geiger counter of any woman I know." I had been sobbing on the phone, telling him how proud he would be of me for what I had done and how sad I was feeling in spite of my wise decision. My dearest friend had turned my tears into abundant laughter. "Edward, you're the best."

When Howard came up to me and introduced himself, towards the end of a professional association Christmas party in mid December, I felt myself swallowed up by his magnetic steel blue eyes. There had been only one other time that I had experienced such an immediate physical reaction to a man; the first time had been when I met my former husband when we were in college. Howard and I primarily discussed business but it was clear how much we were attracted to and interested in each other. Even though it was a rather brief conversation, we quickly learned that we shared several interests and there was a striking similarity in how we thought and what our values were. Howard told me much later that he had actually already left the party, had stopped in the men's room before getting his coat and, for some unidentified reason, had been drawn back into the room again. Neither of us had noticed each other before that. He gave me his business card and said that he would be interested in receiving one of my brochures.

The next day when I addressed my brochure to Howard, I wrote a note inside that said simply, "Tennis in the New Year?" Howard had mentioned that he loved playing tennis and was always looking for a good game. Within a few days I had a phone call from him and we agreed to get together in January for tennis since I was leaving town at the end of that week to spend the holidays with my parents. Just as we were ending the conversation, he mentioned that he would be in Florida for a long weekend over Christmas. Fate seemed to be playing a hand to pull Howard and me together. He was still undecided between two hotel choices; one of them was on the grounds of the complex where my parents lived. When I told him that, he invited me for dinner the day he would be arriving in Florida, Christmas Eve. He also asked if I wanted to play tennis that afternoon.

"So it's happening." I thought as I hung up the phone. For almost two years I had been living with reconstructed breasts and the physical and emotional scars of breast cancer, wanting to come out of my cocoon. It had been cozy inside with my dear companion,

Jake, who had been there solidly for me throughout both my sister's and my own breast cancer journeys. It was so sheltered and safe with him. Yet I was still driven toward venturing out to find a deeper emotional and physical connection with a man, a life partner. At the same time, I was quite uneasy about the prospect of exposing my body's altered identity to anyone new. Breast cancer had robbed me of my natural comfort with physical closeness and my lack of inhibition. It had stolen my ease of entering into new relationships and moving into intimacy.

I still felt sensual and sexual with my bowls, as I called them, but my body was changed and so was I. I had never rejoined or returned to the gym after my surgery. I no longer felt comfortable in the locker room. In the past I had walked easily, dripping wet, from the shower to the sauna and lain there nude without any self-consciousness or repression. I had never even noticed others' nakedness. When my sister, Jodie, had her mastectomy in April of 1990, I started fixating on what other women's naked breasts looked like, as I walked around the locker room. Less than three years later - and only five months after Jodie's death from breast cancer - with my own new unnatural-looking reconstructed breasts, I could not bring myself to return to the gym and lie down naked in the sauna or remove the towel from around my torso in front of others. When I bought a tiny dog to rejoice in my survival from breast cancer and to symbolize my lost breasts, I used going home at lunchtime to take her out, as an excuse not to go to the gym anymore. The truth was that I no longer felt able to go there. My easy unrestrained former self no longer existed.

When Howard and I played tennis that first time together in Florida, I kept wondering if he would notice that my breasts were stationary. The first warm weather day after I had my mastectomy surgery in the winter of 1993, when women were walking down the street without coats or heavy garments to cover their chests, I had watched their bouncing, jiggling breasts moving naturally under their knit shirts and silk blouses, with a flood of unexpected emotion. I had felt anger and even hostility to be deprived of that basic female commodity. I was nostalgically sad to watch the rhythm and movement of their bodies that I no longer had. As I worried what Howard might be thinking and observing about my non-jiggling bust line, I still managed to watch the ball and play tennis decently. It kept feeling so apparent to me that this was the man I could move forward with in my new identity. I felt unsure of my new physical self but so sure of what I wanted to happen.

I selected a favorite restaurant on the Inter-Coastal Waterway for our dinner that night. It was low key and casual. Howard and I both wanted to eat outside even though it was unusually cool and breezy. I was wearing khaki pants, a white cotton man-tailored banded collar shirt buttoned at the neck, a wool gabardine blazer and a long black silk fringed scarf imprinted with multicolored frogs around my neck and down over my lapels. Covered so well and sitting in a restaurant, I had no concern about the appearance or movement of my breasts while we were eating and I could concentrate on getting to know Howard. Again, there was a rich connection in all that we talked about. We laughed easily and shared common thinking on many topics.

After dinner, I suggested we drive to the fishing pier and walk out over the ocean to look at the full moon on the water. Howard unknowingly made an illegal turn into the wrong end of the parking lot at the pier and a sole police officer insisted on giving Howard a ticket for that minor offense. There had been no other cars anywhere at that hour on Christmas Eve. The spirit of the holiday seemed totally shattered but the event deepened Howard's and my connection. I was able to see the attorney interact with the law and he was able to see my communication skills put to the test. Neither of our professional platforms and talents provided any benefit. The cop obviously wanted someone to pay for his having to work on a holiday eve. I worried that my suggestion to drive to the pier and the resulting ticket would sour our beautiful beginning. I could also feel just the opposite happening.

The next day, Howard played golf during the day and accepted an invitation from my mother to join us at my family's holiday party in the evening. He and my mother clicked together easily and he naturally fit in with everyone there. I liked seeing him in that setting.

We agreed to play tennis again in the morning. Afterwards, Howard asked me to drive up the coastline with him to see the surrounding area before he went to the airport. I recognized that those three days gave us much more time together than we would have had at the start if we had been in New York.

We shared a lot about what our lives and dreams were. He learned about my connection to Jake and how much I wanted a deeper more permanent relationship and partnership. He told me that he had never been married and wanted that very much. His biggest regret in life was that he had never fathered a child. He was emotional when he talked about how much he wanted that to happen in his life and how sad he felt that his choices had not led him to those life rewards. I felt concerned about the fact that I was two years older than Howard, had a grown son and was probably in the early stages of menopause. Even though older women were successfully becoming pregnant and delivering healthy babies, I knew that, as a breast cancer survivor, I could not select the route of extreme hormone exposure that those women were choosing. For many years, I had regretted that I had only one child and certainly longed for a greater family existence. I felt more and more drawn to Howard.

When we drove up the coastline, Howard wanted to stop for a stroll on the beach. Phil Collins was singing on the car radio when Howard turned off the ignition: "So hold on my heart. Please tell her to be patient, cause there has never been a time that I wanted something more… So hold on my heart; just hold on to that feeling. We both know we've been here before. We both know what can happen. So hold on my heart." Those lyrics stuck in my head as we walked up the beach together. I could feel Howard's desire growing and knew he would be the man to expose my soul and new breasts to. After about ten minutes' walking and talking, he turned to me and said, "I want to kiss you." My heartbeat was competing with the sound of the rolling surf. Sadly, I was distracted from the passion and purity of that first kiss. I was too concerned about what my hard breasts would feel like to Howard as he kissed me and held me to him.

On the Sunday after New Year's Day back in New York, I was invited to a party at my friend Edward's new apartment. I asked him what he predicted for us in the New Year and he said, "Well, you're going to stay in your comfortable rut and still be with Jake for the year." "I don't think so, Edward. This year is going to be different." He just laughed at me and expressed his doubt. After the party, Howard had invited me to his home to watch football with him. I was excited about seeing him again and nervous. I had not told him about my reconstructed breasts and about my breast cancer.

When I arrived at Howard's apartment, all I wanted to do was take my clothes off. It was a temperature need rather than a sexual one. Having sex with Howard was as far from my being ready for, as my lost breasts were from my body. The weather was bitter cold that day and I was wearing leggings, a mid thigh length sweater and a long scarf, all three in thick fur-blend sweater-knit and all dyed to match in my favorite delphinium bluest purple color. I was dressed for the cold outdoors and needed to shed those warm clothes. Within minutes of being in Howard's home for the first time, I was searching his wardrobe to find comfortable lighter weight clothing to wear to watch football. It felt completely natural to be in his bedroom changing from my clothes into his. I became almost an observer watching myself, with southern charm and ease, walk into a man's home, go through his drawers and put on his sweats and old tee shirt. "So, Cindy, maybe you are still you." I thought to myself. "Maybe breast cancer hasn't robbed you of the dance after all."

When I sat on the couch next to Howard, I kept squirming away from him and repositioning myself so that he could not lean against, brush across, engage in any way, with the front of my upper body. We had kissed on the beach and it would be so sweet to kiss some more. I felt so inhibited and so worried. I kept folding my arms across my chest for protection. I just wanted to tell him my story and end the agony that I was experiencing but no words could find their way out of my mouth on that topic.

After considerable struggle, I finally was able to say that I had something important and difficult to tell him. He was dear and patient as I searched for a comfortable way to describe that I had no real breasts, that I had had four surgeries the previous year, that because of my sister's heroic, horrific and futile fight for her life, I had made dramatic choices when I was diagnosed with breast cancer three months following her death. What if he rejected me? What if he no longer found me desirable? What if he was repelled?

What he was, was darling. "So can I see them?" he asked in the most tender, gentle and warmly humorous way. It was so genuine and so disarming. I had done it! I had told him! And he was still there. He still wanted me. It felt like I had taken a huge and formidable stride. Suddenly what had seemed impossible seemed easy. I still existed. The deep sighs of relief that came out of me were so cleansing and freeing.

Before I changed my clothes to go home, before Howard took me down to the street to get me a taxi, I had sat on that couch with my bare reconstructed breasts against his wonderful hairy chest. Tears of joy and sadness had streamed down my cheeks. I was thrilled to be out of my cocoon. I was also deeply sad that there was zero feeling in my new nipples and breasts.

Howard was actually the first man in my life with a luxuriously hairy chest. My father had an abundance of chest hair and I had always thought that was quite an appealing and sexy feature on a man. I felt so ironically deprived to be finally chest to chest with my dream come true, to be so visually appreciative of the discovered treasure and not be able to have any sensation in the one area where I could most appreciate the value of my find.

Howard and I continued to see each other regularly. We took two trips. We celebrated each of our birthdays together. Howard spent a lot of time with my friends and family. He told me he liked them all a lot and even commented on how he seemed to fit in so easily with them. I found myself telling people, "I'm done. This is it."

Howard did not introduce me to his friends and family. One night, seated at his kitchen table, late night snacking, we were discussing all kinds of unearthly topics from belief in God and life after death to funeral arrangements. He gave me some instructions to be sure to tell his sister in the event of his death. "Howard, how will I tell your sister this? I don't even know her."…

On Valentine's Day at dinner, Howard shared with me an extensive family tree that a cousin had recently researched and sent to him. He spoke of his huge disappointment in being a solo branch with no offspring on that chart. I asked him what his best friends, a couple that he repeatedly told me he wanted me to meet, would say if I asked them why he had never been married. He told me that the man would say that he had had bad luck with women and the wife would just shrug her shoulders and shake her head.

When I fixed breakfast for him on his forty-seventh birthday, he asked me if I would do the same the next year. He always spoke of a future together and he always spoke of his desire to be a father.

In late April, I met Howard at the movies one Friday night. After a late supper we went home to his place. The next morning he told me he had a tennis game that day at the beach where he had a weekend home. We had spent lots of time there together. I was totally shocked when he said he was going without me and that he needed to end our relationship. He made some kind of disturbing statement about how hard it was to live with his choices. When he drove me home, I asked him if he realized how often he had spoken of our being together in the future and he answered, "I guess that was because of how much I wanted it to happen."

On Sunday night he came over to my house to talk about his choice. He had decided that I was too old to become the mother of his children. It was extremely painful to hear him say the words, "I love you." for the first time and know that he was still forcing himself to give me up. I asked him, "So Howard, how often do you think this type of relationship and these kinds of feelings happen between two people?" And he answered, "Not very often; I'd say once every forty-seven years."

For weeks and months I walked around in pain. The tears were so abundant that I became frightened that I would not regain control or get beyond the ache. I had not broken down and cried since my sister's funeral. Tears had fallen from my eyes but I had never truly wept since then. I had not shed a tear when I was told that I had breast cancer. The weeping that followed Howard was mostly residual, from all of the loss I had never allowed myself to grieve. If I had not loved Howard so deeply, I could have appreciated the release of anguish that he provided.

When a dear playmate from high school invited me to meet him in Virginia for his class reunion over July Fourth, I decided the diversion would be wonderful. Old familiar faces and the southern comfort of home sounded ideal for wound licking and spirit lifting. It turned out to be even better than I could have ever imagined. There was someone at the reunion, whom I did not remember knowing at all from high school, who decided to sweep me off my feet. I was easily sweepable and reboundingly ready for a Howard replacement. Ned was bigger than life, a man of extremes. He made me laugh so hard and so much in those few days that I returned to New York amazingly different from when I had left for Virginia.

Ned and I were both starving for a coupled existence and became quickly and passionately intertwined. I continued to be swept away by him and he would ask me to marry him within a month of that reunion.

Before we met, Ned had known that I had breast cancer and significant surgery, because of the close relationship he had with my good friend who had told him my story. So it was much easier the second time to expose my manmade breasts and share intimacy than it had been that football night with Howard. There was no requirement to prepare Ned in advance.

Ned was so respectful of my scars and rebuilt breasts that he challenged me to be more respectful of myself. He did not like it that I put myself down, as he saw it, by calling my reconstructed breasts, "my bowls". "They are your breasts, not your bowls! What makes you say you don't have breasts?" He contributed an awareness of my attitude that I had not previously recognized. He was right. There was a negativity attached to my label. As time passed after that, I still continued to call my new breasts, my bowls, but the term became one of endearment rather than of self-mockery.

Ned was endlessly generous and wildly fun to be with but eventually the extreme quality to his character, that had attracted me so much to him initially, revealed itself in ways that I would come to see as completely undesirable.

When I wrote my numerous holiday greetings in December, I wrote in each, "1995 has been quite tumultuous! I have been madly in love with two attorneys this year. The first one broke my heart and the second was way too extreme for me. I am exhausted and looking forward to a peaceful, uneventful 1996!"

Late one October afternoon in the fall, while waiting for the Second Avenue bus, I noticed a tall thin man in running shorts, a tank shirt and high tech running shoes and I said to him, "I bet you're on your way to The Park to run." "Why don't you come with me?" he answered. "I wish I could; I meant to leave myself enough time to run this morning and I didn't. I have to pick up my dog from the vet before six o'clock." We spoke briefly and I gave him my phone number. He had a charming foreign accent and I sensed his "normalcy" but I still felt quite uncomfortable when I got on the bus. I never gave my home phone number out to anyone other than my close friends and family and I had just given it to a total stranger.

Several days later, I had hung up the phone from an invasive annoying telemarketing call, when the phone immediately rang again. There was a strange voice on the line with an accent somewhere between Gandhi and Count Dracula. I was about to hang up on what I thought was another marketing call when I realized it was my tall stranger from Second Avenue. After talking for a bit, we agreed to meet in Central Park to run together.

We ran for about fifty minutes early the next day and ended up at The Boathouse for muffins and juice. I learned that Jusef was forty-one and had never been married. As we were talking, I noticed his big strong hands and thought how nice it would be to have them touch me. It had been almost a year since my last romantic episode. In 1995, I had been in love twice; I had shared my breast cancer journey with and exposed my reconstructed breasts to two men and neither story had turned out to provide the partnering that its beginning had promised. I had become weary and gun shy of relationships. I had wanted a calm and peaceful 1996 and had created one. I sensed that Jusef would be a good man to play with for a while.

We ran together several more times. We spoke on the phone often. We went to the movies and had dinner afterwards. We met at the Union Square Farmer's Market one Saturday. We sat on a bench in Union Square Park and talked. Jusef told me about how his life had been in danger and he had been forced to flee his country for political reasons, as a young college student. He described his boyhood in a small Eastern European country that I knew by name only. He shared his strong patriotism and I liked his values a lot. He was easy to be with and I instinctively felt safe with him. When I left him in Union Square, knowing that he would be coming to my house for dinner that night, I decided that I would send him an e-mail when I got home. I wrote:

> So I've decided to tell you something very private, using e-mail, that is hard to say in person.
>
> My sister died in September of 1992 of breast cancer.
>
> In December of 1992, I was diagnosed with in situ breast cancer which is classified as Stage Zero (!) and often considered by medical practitioners as pre-cancerous. In situ breast cancer consists of microscopic calcifications that have no blood system and therefore can not involve lymph nodes, be systemic or threaten your life. (At the other end of the spectrum from what my sister's diagnosis was.) After biopsies and medical opinions, I decided to make sure that I would never have to go through what my sister experienced.
>
> In 1993 I had four surgeries.
>
> This is a part of my past that I do not dwell on, yet at the same time I am always aware of what I have been through and how my life has been marked by this experience. Of course, I would never have selected breast cancer if I could have controlled the roll of the dice but somehow what I have gained from my losses is of tremendous value. I have perspective on and an appreciation of life, enormous joy and clarity about what I value and want.

> So enough said on this "lovely" topic via e-mail.
>
> See you later…. C

"What a long way you've come from that first time you told a man that you had had breast cancer!" I reflected to myself. I no longer felt fearful of rejection. I easily and confidently found the words I needed. There was no hesitation. E-mail provided a way to hide any discomfort I would feel giving that information to Jusef face to face. If he were going to reject me, then he could call and cancel dinner, reply by e-mail or just not show up.

When Jusef came to dinner that night, we talked and talked. I continued to like his values and have a positive response to him. I felt comfortable with him. He was such a gentle soul. Whenever I looked at his hands, I wanted to feel their touch. Finally after hours at the dinner table, I stood up, walked around to his side, took his hand and led him over to my living room couch. I wanted to be held by a man I trusted.

Later, as we walked up the stairs to my bedroom, I asked him, "What if I am only doing this because it has been so long since I've done it?" "That's okay." he reassured me.

Jusef and I would be coupled companions for the next eighteen months. My reconstructed breasts had simply become part of my physical apparatus. I no longer yearned for or thought about how it used to be. I had become a new woman with a new physical identity that was totally comfortable for me. Jusef was without question the most affectionate man I had ever known. We were quite compatible together but our backgrounds and life goals were dramatically opposed. Having spent seven years in a prior limited relationship, I became quite restless and disappointed in myself for continuing to stay with Jusef, no matter how kind, loving and respectful he was. It was clear that we were going nowhere and I still wanted more.

When I finally ended my relationship with Jusef, I knew my decision came out of considerable life lessons. I was giving up a connection that was satisfying and pleasurable. My old M.O. was to cling to the past until I had found solid new ground to stand on. In my former life I was focused on immediate temporary gain and unconcerned about longer-term goals. Breast cancer and significant love losses had prepared me well to claim what I wanted and to sacrifice what I currently had, to ensure the kind of future I was seeking.

Widower on the Beach

For years I had had a fantasy about meeting and marrying a widower with two young daughters. When a friend told me about David, my thoughts immediately focused on his widowhood and fatherhood. His wife had died less than a year before of brain cancer and he had twin nine-years-old daughters. David lived in Philadelphia and would be coming to New York periodically for consulting assignments. My friend asked me if I would meet with David to talk to him about the potential of my providing communication coaching to one of David's consulting clients.

In that first meeting over lunch, I felt quite torn. I could easily concentrate on the professional agenda of the meeting but I also was drawn to David on a personal level. He told me that he was considering using another consultant who had been recommended to him as well and deep inside I was hoping that he would select the other person so that he and I could be free to explore a social relationship together.

We agreed to meet again the next day, when I offered to provide David with some specific approaches to a particular challenge that his client was facing. David began flirting with me from the beginning. He spoke openly of his daughters and his deceased wife. He asked me lots of personal questions and learned that my sister had died of breast cancer. He said that he knew I must be vigilant about mammography as a result. I answered his related question in a non-direct way, telling him that I did everything to ensure that women were educated about the benefits of yearly mammograms, without telling him that I no longer had breasts needing mammography. We stuck to business topics but non-business ones were always there on the surface of our conversation.

David and I spoke a few more times on the phone and he let me know that he had chosen me as the communication consultant for the project that he was working on. I had mixed feelings about his decision.

Whenever we would meet he would always talk about personal topics with me. I was quite drawn to him but recognized all of the dangers in my attraction. My friend told me that David had said to her, "All I want to do is marry Cindy and take her home with me."

One day when David had stepped over the line into that male/female dance territory, I said to him, "David, we need to talk." "I know." he replied. When I told him that when we first met over lunch, I had hoped he would choose the other consultant, he looked terribly wounded. He seemed relieved when I said that the reason for my wanting that was because I was personally interested in him and would not pursue that interest if we were working together. I also told him that since then, I had come to realize that it was too soon after his wife's death for him to be involved with another woman anyway and that he was still too raw and vulnerable. "Basically, the best of all worlds is for us to work together professionally and get to know each other on that basis. If, at a later and quite different point in time, we decide to move forward together, we will already have become great friends." I told him that I knew how much emotional pain he was experiencing because of the loss of his wife and that he could stay relaxed and do and say whatever he wanted to with me. I said that I would take responsibility for controlling the parameters of "our deal". That night he left me a sweet voice mail message thanking me for being so aware, for providing him with such a safe haven and for giving him my friendship.

David's consulting client decided not to go forward with the communication portion of the project and I was quite relieved. I continued to meet with David when he came in from Philadelphia on business and I continued to insist that our relationship stay on a business basis. His emotional vulnerability was huge and I knew that if we were going to have any long-term personal relationship or a future together, I needed to protect what was growing between us carefully.

David's special attention to me was constant. He began calling me daily and we would spend lots of time on the phone. He sent me beautiful flowers for my birthday with a card that said, "Dear Cindy, I hope that you have a great day. Please know that I am thinking of you and would like to be with you. Happy Birthday With Hugs, David". We regularly wrote long e-mails to each other. When I went skiing alone in Vermont he called me, worrying about my driving home in a storm. His devotion was enormous. He told me that I had become his anchor. We had dinner or lunch together from time to time when he was in New York working.

Even though I carefully controlled the boundaries of our interactions, my feelings for David were growing tremendously. I became quite clear about what I wanted to happen. I knew that the timing was not right yet and I knew that I needed to be patient.

There was a tiny freckle-like spot just above the top circle of my left implanted breast that kept forming a pinpoint of a scab. Although it was almost imperceptible, I knew that it was more than likely skin cancer from over exposure to the sun when I was younger. When it was confirmed through biopsy as basal cell cancer, I made an appointment with a plastic surgeon to have it removed, knowing exactly the type of scar my body would produce no matter how fine the procedure would be.

Immediately following the minor surgery to remove the freckle and the necessary surrounding tissue, I met David for drinks before he caught his train back to Philly. Somewhere in the back of my mind was a thought about my first scar that marked the removal of a benign fibroid tumor from my left breast. I had always related that scar under my left armpit to a lost love. I pushed the thought away, hoping that I would not have a similar connection to David for the new scar.

Even though the surgery was so totally minor and even though the need for it was miniscule, relative to my other four surgeries to remove and reconstruct my breasts, I was both angry and sad to gain a new scar in such a visibly prominent place. My new breasts were rather unnatural looking and their scars were significant but I had been able to wear any type of clothing that I wanted without any of my breast cancer scars showing. My bust line looked rather natural in low-cut clothing as if I were wearing a pushup bra. There would be no way to wear the type of tops I liked so much and still hide the new mark on my chest …*just over my heart.*

When David and I met for drinks that night he was concerned about my surgery but also seemed much less eager to dwell on it than he had previously wanted to focus on my drive in the snowstorm. I could feel his resistance to hearing about anything medical and I wondered how I would ever be able to tell him my breast cancer story. We quickly changed subjects and talked about our children and what it was like to be a single parent when there were everyday issues related to school and homework.

It turned out that David would be spending a holiday with his daughters at his mother's home located near the resort where I was going to be with my parents to celebrate my mother's eightieth birthday. David and I decided we would see each other there and it felt like we were finally stepping forward a bit in our relationship. We talked about going to the next place together and decided that the neutral location away from our business environment would be right. We continued to speak on the phone daily and I knew it was time to move ahead. And I also knew that it was time to tell David about my breast cancer experience.

We met in the evening and decided to walk on the beach together. The full moon was so bright that it seemed almost like daytime. The air was so warm and the breeze so delicious that it felt exactly like those fragrant tropical nights when I had lived in Nassau that I remembered so dearly.

We had never even hugged each other and we both wanted that so much. There were those hard bowls on my chest that I needed to discuss before hugging. It felt more difficult than ever before to breach that topic with David. I still had all of the comfort I had gained in my new identity. I still felt totally in tune with my new self, but David's wife had died of cancer less than a year before. What if the association was too strong for him? What if he couldn't take in that I had eliminated all threat to my life from breast cancer? I knew it was time to go there, yet I felt as if I had never told a single soul about my having had breast cancer. The stakes were higher than they had ever been before.

David was neither shocked nor repelled when I told him about my breast cancer and reconstructed breasts. We held each other close and we were clearly much more deeply connected than ever before. We stayed on the beach for hours. We talked a lot and there was much silence too as we curled closely together on lounge chairs and listened to the waves breaking on the sand. At some point, I asked David, "How will it be possible to face you in the same professional way when we're back in New York?" "You won't have to. We'll be able to have both parts of our connection from now on."

I returned to New York to learn that my three-days-per-week consulting job had ended abruptly. It was both shocking and devastating but I somehow felt that there was a new door opening that would be significant and satisfying. One of my first thoughts, when I was informed of my loss, had to do with David. I connected being able to move forward with him in a new way, to the end of my job. He was in flight returning home when I received the news. I left him a voice mail message telling him I was all right but that something serious had happened and I needed to talk to him as soon as possible.

When he called and I told him what had taken place, he responded that he would get in his car that minute and drive to New York to be with me. I knew that he had just arrived back home with his girls and I reassured him that I was fine and could see him first thing in the morning since he had business meetings in New York the next day.

I was still in shock from my job disappearance when David rang my doorbell. He was so tender and caring about my pain and loss. Somehow everything became quite disorienting. I actually felt completely numb when he took me in his arms. All of my desire from our night on the beach was gone. It was I who was needy for the first time. And even though he had come to comfort me, he actually couldn't handle my being vulnerable and less than the strong, clear, self-sufficient woman with whom he had come to feel so safe. We left my house together to go to two separate meetings and I could almost reach out and touch how different he was, as we walked up Fifth Avenue together.

As time passed, I would be less and less in contact with David. We met for dinner one night and he clearly conveyed to me, without saying the finalizing words, that he could not move forward with me.

It hurt so much losing my job and that wonderful relationship, both so highly treasured, simultaneously. I would never know which event had pushed David away: learning that I had had breast cancer or seeing me vulnerable without employment. Perhaps, it was the combination of the two. Perhaps it was something altogether different.

I knew I would survive the pain. I decided to hike the Grand Canyon with a dear friend to celebrate my invincibility and mourn my losses.

Young Runner

At the beginning of a seminar I was attending outside of Chicago, I asked the participants if there was anyone who would like to run with me the following morning. I had been told at the hotel concierge desk that it was unsafe for women to run alone there. During the first break, I was pleased when a young man from Arizona named Dan came up to me and said he'd like to join me the next day to run.

At the end of the day, I queried the group again to see who was going into Chicago for dinner that night. There were two invitations to go with people to those well-known commercial restaurants that every tourist *must* go to and which we had in New York. I had never been to either and certainly had no desire to go to one of them in Chicago. It was again quite pleasing when Dan came up to me and asked me to join him and some of his colleagues for dinner in Chicago. "We want to go to someplace local and non-touristy", he said. It was just what I wanted to hear.

That night was terrific fun and exactly what I needed. I had just turned fifty the preceding week and had been through two painful, passionate and extremely disappointing romances that year. My last expectation or desire was to be without a man in my life when I turned fifty but there I was - alone and rather gun shy and exhausted from what had been going on in my life. I just wanted to laugh and have fun. And so I found myself riding the El train into Chicago with three probably under thirty-year-olds. What a hoot that night was! We ate Spanish food in a tapas restaurant, ordering plate after plate of exotic dishes accompanied by pitchers of sangria and taking turns covering the tab. That was followed by a drinking contest and tons of laughter in a bar where we played a great game called Pass the Pigs. Then it was on to dancing at a club. Dan and I danced and laughed and danced and laughed. That night the four of us told each other more dirty jokes than I had ever heard in my life. I was certainly old enough to be the mother of any one of them but unquestionably I had the highest energy level and the most fun of the whole group. The laughter lasted all the way home on the train.

Somehow even after that just-what-the-doctor-ordered, fun-filled, alcohol-filled night, I was still able to get up to meet Dan in the lobby of the hotel the next morning to run at 6:00 a.m.

Since running provided such a great way to talk and get to know a companion runner, Dan and I shared a lot about ourselves that morning. After we reviewed our wild and crazy evening together and laughed some more about it all, I told him about the two men I had been in love with that year and how heartbroken I had been. He told me about a committed relationship he had been in that was over and how much he wanted to have another serious relationship but that all the girls he met wanted only to have fun. It was obvious that he certainly wasn't opposed to having fun; it was just that he wanted more.

Even though we were running a few miles from O'Hare Airport in a fairly densely populated and highly commercial area, the trail was surrounded by thick woods. A deer came onto the path, staring at us as we approached her, and finally leaped off into the trees. We talked about our mutual love of the outdoors: hiking, fishing, skiing. I learned that Dan had done a considerable amount of trekking, had worked as a white water guide and had been camping in almost all of the State parks.

We had been running for over a half an hour when I commented that in spite of some significant losses that I had experienced, I still believed that life was wonderfully enthralling and that I wouldn't trade anything for all that I had learned along the painful way. He emphatically reinforced my sentiments, saying how profoundly he, too, had learned to appreciate life in that way. Dan was twenty-eight with cropped blond hair and mischievous blue eyes; he looked like he was about seventeen. When he responded in such a mature and experienced way, I wanted to reach out and pat him on the head, thinking, "Now what could this innocent-looking young boy know about loss?"

It was hard to participate in the seminar that second day, with those three playmates from the night before in the room. Every once in a while, one of them would make a comment to the entire group that cleverly but discreetly referenced an event or joke from the night before. I felt invigorated to be so full of life professionally and personally that day, with almost no sleep the night before, and with some significant losses and a major birthday spent uncoupled, so closely preceding.

There was a severe hale storm in Chicago that day, damaging many airplanes, and O'Hare was experiencing endless flight delays. Dan, a few others from the seminar and I spent hours together at the airport, drinking, laughing, eating junk food and exchanging e-mail addresses.

One of the conversations, amongst that diverse group of unlikely companions, had centered on the new blue M&M. I had voiced my decided opposition to this break with a comforting childhood tradition. Later when I boarded my plane, I put my hand into my coat pocket and found a single blue M&M. It would always bring a smile to my face and would be kept as a valuable treasure on a glass shelf, nestled among multi-colored worn smooth pieces of beach glass.

It was clear that Dan and I had a tremendous affinity for each other and had definitely become connected. We began speaking frequently on the phone and became e-mail buddies. Within a few weeks of our time in Chicago, I asked Dan what he was doing that weekend. He told me he was a bit nervous about taking a young boy fishing whom he hadn't seen for over a year. As I asked a few more questions, I learned that Dan had lived with the boy and his mother who had committed suicide. Dan had come home one day with flowers and groceries to cook dinner for her, and found her dead in their bed. To add to his anguish, the woman's parents had kept Dan from the funeral and had prohibited the son from seeing Dan.

As I listened to him express his deep emotions over this bitter experience, I thought about that day when we were running and I had felt so smug and patronizing. It was clear that he was mature and aware much beyond his years and appearance. I was deeply touched by his depth of feeling and experience, and was rather ashamed of my pre-conceived misjudgment.

Eventually I shared with Dan my reactions to him at those two separate points in time. I also finally told him about my sister's dying from breast cancer, the role of breast cancer in my life and how I had given up my breasts. Our bond became deeper.

As time passed we often were in contact and at other times we seldom wrote or spoke. A considerable amount of our communication was about our individual love lives. We talked and wrote easily about sex, about the differences between men and women, and about our own dreams and longings.

A little over a year later, I experienced two more devastating losses: another man, a widower, whom I had developed deep feelings for and my job! For two months I poured myself into rebuilding my life and found another three-days-a-week perfect position which would allow me to continue with my private practice and other activities and would give me the kind of freedom and flexibility that I craved. When I had lost my other job, I never dreamed I would be able to obtain another three-day position at the professional level and with the challenge that I was accustomed to. The new one was going to be even better!

When I had simultaneously lost my job and the man, I had decided that I needed to see The Grand Canyon before beginning anew. I wanted to have a significant challenge to conquer and own, that would represent my dauntless courage and ability to take life on with all of its relentless attacks and disappointments. I wanted to celebrate life and I wanted to celebrate the beauty of the earth. I had seen the Grand Canyon from an airplane window and had always wanted to see it up close and personal. My sister had been there shortly before she had been diagnosed with breast cancer and had raved about its beauty.

The day I received my new job offer, I called Dan and left him a voicemail message, "Are you okay? It has been a while since we've been in touch. Will you go to the Grand Canyon with me?

Are you finally running the New York Marathon this year?" The phone rang while I was eating dinner that night. "Yes, yes and maybe." he began. Then, "We're going to hike The Grand Canyon on August first, all the way down and all the way back up in one day! And the next day we're running a half marathon." All the laughter we had always shared came tumbling across the phone lines. "You may be running a half marathon the next day but I doubt if I will!" I hadn't even known exactly where The Grand Canyon was and so had not realized that it was practically in Dan's backyard. And to hike it down and back up in one day, that was just the kind of goal I was looking for!

On July 31st, Dan picked me up at the Phoenix airport at around 6:30 p.m. After hugging for several minutes, we jumped in his truck and headed towards The Grand Canyon. We stopped for Mexican food and the dry heat of the desert baked immediately to the core of my bones as soon as we got out of the air conditioning. It felt just right being there and so right being there with Dan.

After dinner, as we continued our drive, I watched the light fade on that stark landscape and marveled at the wonder and diversity of nature. That night we slept in the open air a few miles outside of the park entrance to The Grand Canyon. Dan had driven completely off-road, winding his way through trees and low ground cover. "Is this okay?" he asked. I was ecstatic. He threw a sleeping bag on the ground for himself and showed me my bed inside the back of the truck. He handed me a flashlight and indicated, "Here's your bathroom." pointing into the darkness in front of the truck. "And here's mine." motioning to the area on the other side of his sleeping bag. "Do you want me to close the back of the truck for you?" he asked. "Definitely not!" I replied. I crawled up into my little room and took all of my clothes off in the night blackness. Sleeping naked on that mattress in that sleeping bag, listening to the night sounds and looking out at endless sky and stars was heavenly. I gently spoke out to my companion on the ground. "I may be too excited to sleep."

Around 3:30 in the morning, I woke up and heard what I hoped was Dan rustling around on the ground outside of my abode.

Finally one of us spoke, "Are you awake? Shall we get up now?" And so we drove into the park before daybreak and watched the sun rise on The Grand Canyon, eating raisin bran cereal at the rim with surprisingly only a handful of other people in the vicinity.

Pilgrimage to the Grand Canyon

August 1, 1997

-South Rim: Arrival before daybreak, following a night under the stars, sleeping in a truck. Glorious!

-Sunrise at the rim with raisin bran.

-7:30 a.m. Kaibab trail: Seven miles down. Steep. No water on trail. Look!

-Phantom Ranch at bottom by 11:30 a.m. 112 degrees! Lemonade!

-Begin Bright Angel trail: 1:40 p.m. Nine miles up with water stops.

-Back at rim: 7:50 p.m.

~~~~~~~~~~~~~~~~~~~~~~~

A daunting challenge. The sense of not having what it takes to do it.

The knowledge and conviction that it can and will be done.

IN ONE DAY! IN STIFLING HEAT! YES!

The beauty of it all!

Look! Look! Look!

The ever-changing landscape.

The vastness! The vistas! It goes on and on and on. Each perspective adds to the appreciation. Each step taken teaches the significance of "one step at a time".

The colors! The wonder! It IS Grand!

Two thirds of the way back up, I asked Dan, "Did we do the Grand Canyon? - or - Did the Grand Canyon do us?" Dan answered, "Ask the question again when we're back up at the top!"

~~~~~~~~~~~~~~~~~~~~~~~~

Both are true.

I *DID* The Grand Canyon:
-I set the goal - for its challenge, for its beauty, for its satisfaction.

-I chose an experienced guide whom I liked and trusted. A friend.

-I prepared - I ran hard and long every day for weeks before I went. I took plenty of food and water. I wore the right clothes and shoes. I covered myself in sunscreen. I went slowly. I rested.

-I used it for a symbol for life. I took pain and loss with me and *left* them there. I brought the solitude, peacefulness and self-reliance that I gained there away with me - to keep with me.

-I *knew* I could do it.

-I *wanted* to do it.

-I readied myself for the challenges ahead.

~~~~~~~~~~~~~~~~~~~~~~~~

The Grand Canyon *DID* me:
-It showed me my insignificance.

-It assaulted my body and my strength.

-It mocked my attempts to surround myself with beauty.

-It belittled my sense of time and urgency.

-It laughed at possessions.

-It humbled me and left me in awe.

-I am changed forever from its grandeur.

~~~~~~~~~~~~~~~~~~~~~~~

Life is a series of challenges. The harder they are, the more we can gain from them.

Perspective, attitude and how we cope with challenge are the keys. We are always in control of these, no matter how much happens that is out of our control.

Mourn losses and *LET GO.*
Take charge of your life and *MOVE ON.*

See life as a Grand Canyon, knowing you can master its challenges but can never be its master.

~~~~~~~~~~~~~~~~~~~~~~

I wrote about The Grand Canyon for the widower who had relentlessly pursued me and then had suddenly disappeared from my life as soon as I lost my job. I wrote about The Grand Canyon to grieve my losses and to celebrate my blessings. I wrote about The Grand Canyon to commemorate significant life passages. I wrote about The Grand Canyon as a gift to my sister who was no longer able to relish the magnificence of our planet. I wrote about The Grand Canyon to pay homage to its overwhelming beauty. I wrote about The Grand Canyon to capture it with lasting words and challenge my mortality.

The following day Dan did run a half marathon and I ran only the 5K portion of the race. For the next two days neither of us could take a step without a bit of moaning. We drove off road through the red rock canyons outside of Sedona and stayed in a wonderful bed and breakfast in Jerome. The room we stayed in there had a sign on the door that said, "Sat 'n Spurs". The bed in the room was so tall that when you stood next to it, the top of the bed was at the level of your armpits; you needed a ladder to get into it. We looked like tiny children next to it and both of us broke into hysterical laughter each time we saw the other one beside it. I read "The Alchemist" to Dan before going to sleep each night and during the daytime drive when I could allow myself to take my eyes from the breathtaking Arizona scenery.

Dan and I would go skiing in Utah together the following February and he would finally run the New York City marathon in 1998 and thrill to his first visit to the Apple. When he came to New York I took him to Mohonk Mountain House in New Paltz to climb boulders, conquer the Crevice (several hundred feet of extremely narrow vertical space between huge rock faces) and see seven States from Skytop tower. After spending the day in magnificent mountainous autumn splendor, we drove back to the City to catch the last glimpse of scarlet sunset from the top of The Empire State Building.

Dan always seemed to be there for me following loss. We had certainly spent a lot of fun and spectacular time together. We shared a deep bond that combined man/woman, boy/girl, sister/brother and even mother/son feelings. Through this relationship, I knew that I would have a valued friend for life. And through it, I also came to understand that the traditional life-partnered romantic and sexual coupled existence that I sought and intensely wanted was not the only way to share and enjoy life with a man.

Totally Sixteen

It had been a long time since I had flown into my hometown.
After years of driving to Virginia from New York, it was striking
to look down from the airplane and see my Star City wrapped in
its surrounding mountainsides. I lovingly thought, "Oh look; it's a
baby town."

On a previous visit, nineteen years prior, I had flown in for my
grandmother's ninetieth birthday and written:

In Flight
Mamaw's Birthday
October 26, 1979

In flight, high above rusty velour mountains spread
out below like a relief map:

> -I smile as I feel the old sense of security and
> peace these mountains have always given me.
> -I laugh as I look at them and see them as a herd
> of wrinkled elephants lazing in the sun.
> -We descend and I see the brightest orange trees
> speckled against the velvet russet in contrast to
> the surrounding aristocratic green fields, long
> since void of spring's new brightness.
> -Each little house and farm captures the sunlight
> and turns into a jewel nestled in the royal cloth
> around it.
> -Now the apparition of the elephants fades as the
> majesty of the mountains rises up from the
> ground below.

We are descending and the smoothness seen from
higher gives way to rugged outlines rounded by time.
– *My mountains* – I'm coming home.

A business trip to North Carolina was providing a means for me to
spend the last weekend of May at home in Virginia to celebrate
my cousin Harry's fiftieth birthday. That Friday night, Harry and
I attended a fundraising event for the city's fine arts center. I was
able to wander through a museum exhibit that was opening in June

to honor the history of the Jewish community in that small city where I grew up. There were numerous exhibits and lots of pictures of my family members and people in the community whom I had known, as a young girl. It was quite moving to see my great uncle's bar mitzvah photograph and my grandmother seated with other young women as members of the first reading club.

I even found a group picture, taken in the country at a tree-planting event, which contained all of the Jewish children I had grown up with. It was challenging locating and recognizing everyone in that photograph. My sister Jodie was there at around age sixteen. I wanted to travel back in time into that picture to warn her and protect her from her future battle with and defeat by breast cancer.

In the photograph, I was standing between my best friends, Jolene and Marilyn. Jolene's mother would die of breast cancer a few years after that photograph was taken and, as a married woman and mother, Jolene would elect bilateral breast removal, as I would also later choose, to protect herself from the end that her mother suffered. That Sunday I would be seeing Marilyn in Durham while there for business. I was filled with emotion as I looked at that slice of life from a gentler time.

Harry and I had a difficult challenge, locating him in the photograph, but finally succeeded. "You know you're old when you find yourself in a museum exhibit!" Harry commented. I felt so aware of what a moving and nostalgic evening I was experiencing to begin that special weekend.

The next morning I found myself alone in a sea of people, waiting for a 5K/10K race to begin. Harry was at the front of the pack, because of his running speed, and I was checking out the guys around me to see if I recognized anyone and to look for available attractive men. About twenty feet ahead of me I saw a tall, quite handsome man with thick dark hair graying at the temples who looked about thirty-five or forty years old. I thought to myself, as I checked to see that he was *not* wearing a wedding ring, "Oh, he's cute; hmmm, he looks a lot like someone I went to high school with; no, wait a minute, that *is* Jesse Baxter!" Then I saw that he was with three other guys I knew from high school. Next to him was Jeb Maitland whom I recognized immediately. Of the other two, I knew exactly who one was but could not find his name in my memory file. The fourth was a bafflement to me; I wasn't even sure that he was someone I had known before. I could not get myself to speak to them. I wasn't sure why. It felt like a combination of

> -that teenage intimidation of not knowing what to say to boys
> -embarrassment from not remembering all of their names
> -loss of breath from the reaction I was having to seeing Jesse Baxter
> -little interest in these southern boys from my past

I overheard them talking and heard them point out a woman standing behind me by her name. It was someone from my class whom I had always liked a lot. Her mother had died of breast cancer in our junior year of high school. I wanted to reach out to her and turned around to say hello. There were only two people I had known who had had breast cancer when I was growing up, both mothers of close friends of mine, and within less than twenty-four hours of being in my hometown, I had haphazardly crossed the paths of both. It was wonderful to greet and speak to that former classmate. The race began as we were reminiscing and catching up with each other and I soon told her that I realized I was keeping her from those she was running with and that I also knew my pace was probably too slow for her; we parted company.

As I solitarily continued the race, I started thinking about those guys. Finally I retrieved from my archives the name I had been unable to remember and also realized exactly who the fourth one was. Now I was prepared to speak to them if I saw them again.

After the point where the 10K portion of the race continued on in one direction and the 5K part that I was running looped back to the beginning, I saw Jeb Maitland and Bennett Raines just ahead of me. Jesse Baxter and Miller Thompson were not with them. I ran along side of the two and said, "It seems to me that a couple of old guys like you could be running a bit faster than this." They flirted back with me for a bit before I called them by their names. They both were rather surprised and asked, "So who are you?" They were happy to see me and we chatted some more before I ran out ahead of them.

When I got back to the bridge, which was rather steep, I began to slow my pace again. Jeb Maitland caught up with me and we continued on together for a while. Jeb told me that he came to New York with his wife and a group of friends every December. I told him to be sure to contact me when he was there.

I began to lose steam a bit and was looking for my cousin Harry who had told me that he would double back and finish the race with me; I did not see him anywhere. Jeb said he would stay with me for the rest of the race. When we saw the finish line we put on some speed and crossed it together. Soon after we finished the race, Bennett Raines joined us but I never saw Jesse Baxter again that day. I did make sure that Jeb knew what my last name had become and how to spell it so that he could look me up in the phonebook and call when he and his wife were in New York the following December.

When I was leaving to find Harry, Jeb said something to me again about old times and how good it was to see me. I replied that when he and I had crossed that finish line together, I had been aware of the fact that he had been the first boy I had ever kissed. I realized what a sweet circle of life we had just completed. He said, "Well, I've certainly always had a warm spot in my heart for you, Cindy."

I got tremendous mileage out of that morning. I immediately called Roberta, my best friend from high school, who had been with me every inch of the way, as I lost my breasts to breast cancer and had my heart broken so many times over the years. Roberta was more than a sister to me and we squealed in joy and disbelief together as I told her about how gorgeous and young Jesse Baxter looked and about finishing the race with Jeb

Maitland, my first-kiss boyfriend. As soon as I finished my conversation with Roberta, I called Marilyn to tell her the same and make plans for dinner together in Durham the next night. Wherever I went that day in the Star City, I played the story for all that it was worth. I kept thinking, "Imagine coming home from the Apple and crossing the finish line of a race in your hometown at age fifty-two with the first boy you ever kissed at age fourteen!. Not bad for amusement and pleasure!"

The work in Durham went well. Marilyn and I, who had known each other since birth, joyously reminisced. Whenever we were together, giggles poured out of us as if not a single day had passed since we were young girls. Marilyn and Jolene were still in close touch with each other since Jolene lived nearby in North Carolina. Marilyn gave me an article from the newspaper about Jolene and the full life she was living, following her courageous and wise decision to remove her breasts prophylacticly.

When I returned to New York on Monday night, I called Roberta in Rhode Island to check in routinely with her and to review once again my running into the "boys" from high school. I also called Marilyn to do the same and tell her how great it was to spend time together again. Mostly I wanted to get some more mileage out of how delicious Jesse Baxter had looked. I felt so appreciative of having such old dear friends to share my life with.

It was about nine o'clock in the evening when I got off of the phone and decided to go into my home office to check my answering machine for messages one last time that day. The light was blinking and I actually started squealing when I heard the following message, "Hey, Cindy, this is Jesse Baxter. Bennett and Jeb told me they saw you at the race on Saturday. I looked for you afterwards but never found you. Jeb told me how to get in touch with you. I'm here in New York on business this week. Here's my number. Give me a call and maybe we can get together. Maybe you can show me around the City."

I rushed back to the other phone and called Roberta and Marilyn again, one after the other. "Listen to this; you won't believe who just called me." I was totally sixteen. "What do you mean you can't call him?" Marilyn asked. "You speak to senior executives all the time and are the most confident person I know!" It was rather absurd but I felt exactly like I was in high school again. Jesse Baxter had been one of the "cool" guys. I couldn't remember if I had ever even spoken to him before and I felt paralyzed and so ineptly young. Marilyn said. "You HAVE to call him, Cindy….Tonight!"

It took a while for me to collect the courage I needed to dial his number and when I did, the hotel employee who answered the phone said, "Good evening. This is The Inn, where your satisfaction is guaranteed." I asked for Jesse's room and when he said hello, I asked without any greeting or self-identification, "So what kind of a place are you staying in, where your satisfaction is guaranteed?!"

It was amazing how easily that conversation started and how my paralysis immediately disappeared. We actually spoke for an hour and a half. We talked about everything. At some point while we were on the phone and completely within the context of what we were discussing, I had told Jesse Baxter that my sister had died of breast cancer, that I had had breast cancer and that I had had both breasts removed and reconstructed. There was such ease in the telling. These were simple basic facts about my life and I had not had a single fear or hesitation in sharing them. It didn't even register as an important event until after I had hung up the phone and suddenly realized the significance of what had just happened. For the first time since my year of surgery, I had told a man about my having had breast cancer at the onset of our first conversation with each other and I had not even thought about his reaction or response. The words came out of my mouth as easily as if I was describing how much I liked to ski or play tennis. "This is good." I thought and exhaled deeply.

Jesse and I did the Apple for the next three days. It did not start out at all romantically. We were just two people who had known each other peripherally when we were growing up. We shared a certain history, timeframe and experience in common that gave us wonderful mutual ground to get to know each other quickly. We spoke of quite similar reactions to each other, both present and past, and neither of us expected those three days to be more than a friendly encounter between old acquaintances. We ate dinner in my garden one night and went to a wonderful restaurant another. We went to the top of The Empire State Building and ran the reservoir in Central Park. We danced to Eric Clapton's new CD in my living room and we fell asleep side by side on my living room couch. When we woke up I asked Jesse if he would have still done spoons with me if we had had sex. He made a darling joke, asking me if I had wanted to have sex, and then asked me what doing spoons was?

The intensity of feeling that evolved for each other, after those three days, was electric and deliciously surprising. We had miles between us that deepened our connection and augmented our desire to be together again. If we weren't e-mailing each other, we were on the phone. Jesse sent me a package with only two spoons nestled in it and I sent him two Top Ten lists:

Top Ten Reasons Why Getting to Know Someone Long Distance Is Wonderful

10. You pay attention to who the person is rather than what the person looks like.
9. You get to eliminate a lot of the distracting powerful effects of chemistry/electricity.
8. You don't have to share your food.
7. You can do whatever you want without making choices to please someone else.
6. You can communicate through wonderful thoughtful e-mails, letters and voicemail messages.
5. You can share a nonphysical deeper intimacy.
4. Your self-sufficiency and independence get all the space they need.
3. You have lots of free time.
2. You can spread out across the entire bed at night.
1. There is no physical contact to cloud your thinking.

Top Ten Reasons Why Getting to Know Someone Long Distance SUCKS

10. You forget what the person looks like.
9. You think you imagined the chemistry/electricity.
8. You can't share your food.
7. You have to run alone.
6. E-mail, letters and the telephone just don't get it.
5. There's no one else but you to clean up the mess you make.
4. You have lots of free time to decide spontaneously what you are in the mood to do at the last minute, and are much more likely to end up alone doing nothing.
3. You lose lots of sleep staying up late at night because you don't like going to bed alone.
2. You can't do spoons together.
1. There is no physical contact.

What grew between us was so in tune and so connected that it was quite overpowering. I traveled to Virginia again several times to be with Jesse and I met Jesse for long weekends in two different cities where he was working. He came back to New York for business a couple of times and we took a wonderful vacation trip together. We ran for miles and played tennis for hours. Our physical connection was magical. We viewed the world quite similarly and shared important values in common. We made glorious memories together.

I began to write again in ways I had almost forgotten how. It had been years since I had written poetry:

Awareness

you ride the surface of my awareness

with unimagined lightness

like a rare exotic silken feather

weightless and delightful

tickling my senses with pleasure

and filling my longing with peacefulness

Your Name

alone i sleep
wrapped in the contentment
of your presence

nocturnal rhythms
rouse me from my slumber
and i repeat your name aloud
to the still and empty night
more easily and required
than breathing

Lake Huron

the pearl water curls in whispers to the sand
lake mother soothing her restless child
hush, hush
hypnotic silken sounds
like milkweed brushing the hair of angels

After a wonderful weekend together in Michigan in early October, I realized that what had been so mutual and in sync between Jesse and me had clearly fallen out of balance. I wanted a life partner. I wanted a coupled life. Jesse wanted to make memories with me and would cherish those memories more than if they were made of pure gold but he needed to withdraw into his shell and I could feel it. When I began to tell him on the phone the next week that I needed to disconnect from him and wanted to protect myself from pain, I could hear his heart breaking. I could also feel his sense of freedom and relief to be cast back into the private, comfortable, low-maintenance world that he had built for himself and felt so comfortable in.

I had never felt so sad or so strong. There was a last shred of neediness that I had deeply wanted to cast off and had finally shed by giving up Jesse. I saw how much I had gained from all those physical and emotional scars from my past and I saw that I could stand alone, give up what was so precious to me and know that without total mutuality in a relationship, there was nothing to hold onto.

Knowing how strong the link between Jesse and me was, I was confident that we would find our way back to each other in some form. I needed to be true to myself, first and foremost, and I knew, more surely than ever before, the power of giving up great treasure to get what you want most.

To Life

To Life

In the spring of 1998, five and a half years after my breast cancer diagnosis, I ran the *Race for the Cure* in Central Park. It was a glorious day and I was quite moved to be participating with thousands of women and many breast cancer survivors. It was invigorating and emotional to be running with the distinctive hot pink hat and hot pink background color for the numbers on my chest, designating me as one of the breast cancer survivors running that day. On my back, a sign was pinned that said, "In memory of my sister, Jodie". There was much pride for those of us wearing that hot pink color so publicly and so visibly on our chests. I felt admiration and esteem for all those women who were my sisters that day as we shared the common thread of surviving breast cancer and I also experienced boundless respect for the male survivors who were running in the race.

When the race was over, there were many promotional and educational booths for the runners. Entering the Survivors' tent took me into another world where an exclusive sisterhood existed. I recognized how far we had come from the days when I was a girl and no one ever said the word, cancer, much less went out in public with hot pink signs and hats announcing one's survival from it. The numbers of survivors in 1998 was astounding compared to the usual death sentence of breast cancer when I was young. My joy in being alive was enormous. My sadness for my sister was also ever present.

As I walked around the Survivors' tent I became shocked at how many of the women in their twenties and thirties there were. I tried to calm myself by recognizing that this was a race and not a mere walk or demonstration. Naturally there were going to be many more young women there for that reason than there would be at another type of venue. Somehow that didn't satisfy or calm me. I tried to remember how big New York City was and that there would always be large proportions of every type of individual represented in the great Apple. There was no soothing in that thought either. There were simply too many young women there to be acceptable. Then I realized how many more young breast cancer victims and survivors there were who were not runners or were simply not there that day. I became infuriated at the horror of a disease that strikes so randomly and so viciously.

When I was diagnosed with breast cancer, I had been married and was a mother. I had been through divorce and had been a single woman for years. My ease of dating and entering new relationships was well established. My sexuality and my sexual identity were seasoned and comfortable. When I realized how difficult it still was for me to experience breast cancer and begin dating and face intimacy after mastectomy, my heart began to ache for all of those young women I saw in that tent that day.

It was disturbing that there were so many of them, attacked by breast cancer in the prime of their young womanhood. I knew that, as I had, they would gather strength and, by living with the challenges of breast cancer, that they too would become better women, better lovers, better wives and better mothers. I felt the fears and struggles many would have as single scarred women coping with their sense of diminishment in the search for a mate. I realized also that many of them would not survive. I wanted to reach out to them and give them my support, give them my perspective, tell them how much anger I felt that they had to endure so much suffering and hardship.

As I continued to marvel at their numbers in that tent, I began to formulate how I could touch their lives and bring them comfort and support. In the recesses of my consciousness, I started to formulate how I could write about my own experiences as a gift to those young women and the world. Later in the summer that concept gained a name and structure, and by the next fall, it would emerge, be recorded, take on life.

There are so many messages and insights I have gained that I want to share with others. I know that advice is rarely well received and that soapboxes and preaching turn more people away than attract them. When I was in the fifth grade, my mother received a call from my teacher to say that I was too bossy. There was always that tendency to tell people what to do or how to do it. It started with my sister who never seemed aware of how to succeed, of how to please people or how to protect herself. I watched and learned and became acutely attentive as to how to do otherwise. I always sought to help her, and then everyone else, to see those paths and choices that were so obvious to me. I always wanted to save others from pain and trouble. I always desired to share those life lessons and messages that I had learned through my own awareness, observation, challenge or failure.

The day may never come when breast cancer is alleviated from the earth, but I will do whatever I can in my own way, to contribute to that cause.

Messages

Breastless Intimacy
Outrageous

Soon after my sister was diagnosed with breast cancer, I was
speaking with a friend who was in her early fifties. Her brother
had died of cancer several years before. One of her closest friends
had been fighting breast cancer for almost a decade and was in the
final stages of her battle. I naturally assumed that my friend was
doing all of the various healthcare testing that was needed for
early cancer detection and subsequent cure. I asked her when she
had last had a mammogram and she told me that she had never had
one. I was shocked and asked her how she had made such a
choice. Her answer was simple and regrettably more common
than I wanted to think possible, "If I have cancer, I don't want to
know." None of my logic or pleas made any difference to her
thinking. She had chosen to be an ostrich and nothing I could say
was going to change her decision.

Four years later, another friend, who was in her late forties and
who had lost a sister to cancer in childhood, would also tell me she
had never had a mammogram. She had attended a panel
discussion where I was speaking publicly with other breast cancer
survivors and medical experts. She had told me afterwards that
she had something that she needed to tell me. I knew how difficult
it was for her to say to me that she had never had a mammogram.
For the previous four years, I had been "Mammogram Crusade
Queen", since my sister's diagnosis, death and then my own breast
cancer experience. She asked me to make an appointment for her
and to go with her to get her first mammogram, which I did.
When a year passed, she chose not to get another mammogram.

One night at a party, a woman shared with me that her best friend
had just been told that she had only weeks left to live. The dying
woman had been too terrified to seek help or tell anyone when she
had first felt a lump in her breast. To hide the potential of her
husband's finding out about the lump, she had discontinued all
sexual intimacy with him even though they had always shared a
wonderful physical and sexual relationship throughout their long
marriage. She had also decided to keep the secret because they
had no health insurance benefits; she had not wanted the family to

incur further financial strains. And besides all of that, there had never been anyone in her family who had had breast cancer.

My sister Jodie had made a decision to use her internist for her gynecological needs because she didn't like it that the waiting rooms of gynecologists were filled with pregnant women and often their screaming babies and toddlers. She also didn't like gynecological practices because these doctors were often unable to keep appointments with her whenever they had a patient in labor. She felt that gynecologists placed too high an importance on their obstetric practices. Rather than seek a gynecologist without an obstetric practice or change her extreme perceptions, she had chosen to let her internist prescribe hormone replacement therapy for her. These views, preferences and decisions may have cost her her life. She was fifty years old when she started taking hormones. At that point, it had been a year and five months since she had had a mammogram. She had been taking hormones for seven months when she was diagnosed with breast cancer.

FACTS:

-Mammography can detect early stage, non-palpable, microscopic breast cancer.
-Early detection of breast cancer clearly saves lives.
-The vast majority of breast cancer (not 100%) is detectable through mammography.
-Mammography saves lives.
-Yearly mammography is recommended by many medical experts for women over the age of forty and definitely recommended by all for women over fifty.
-Some types of hormone replacement therapy are associated with stimulation of breast cell growth.
-Hormones can definitely "feed" existing cancer, causing it to grow at a much faster rate, and can greatly increase its virulence.
-***In eighty-five percent of all breast cancer, there is no family history.***

Outrageous! It was outrageous to hear that women were making decisions that could result in their experiencing advanced disease and even unnecessary deaths. It was outrageous that my sister, a medical professional herself, made such life threatening choices. It was beyond outrageous that her internist put her on hormones when it had been over a year since her last mammogram and she had already turned fifty.

How frighteningly outrageous that so many think they don't need screening and that it won't happen to them because there is no history of breast cancer in their families!

How utterly outrageous that many more women and physicians will continue to make these same kinds of perilous decisions!

Each time I experienced loss, I gained powerful new insights and came to value, in new ways, what I had. After my sister's death from breast cancer, and my own bilateral mastectomies, breast reconstruction and numerous heartbreaks - no matter how severe and deep the pain of loss - I learned that I would heal and I would survive. I took great pride in how open, unenvious and unjudging I remained, in spite of all my scars. It became quite easy and wonderfully humorous to create a list of men to stay away from, even though I stood firmly on a foundation that espoused having an open mind, an unbiased viewpoint and an ever-welcoming spirit:

Men to Stay Away From

-Married men

-Alcoholics

-Recovering alcoholics who still have extreme and addictive
 behaviors

-Just divorced men

-Men in the process of getting a divorce

-Attorneys

-Men over forty, who have never been married

-Recently widowed men, seeking a carbon copy of the former
 wife

-Men who say, "I don't want to hurt you. I don't want to break
 your heart."

-Men who say, "I really like being alone."

-Men who say they are falling in love with you and never
 introduce you to the family

-Men who use money to control the world / men who want to
 own you

-Men who live with their mothers

-Men who say, "I'm just not a forever kind of guy."

It Takes Time

A dear friend often soothed others who felt frustrated about their inability to resolve problems, answer questions or achieve goals. She would say,

> "Look, you have to learn to be patient and more self-tolerant. Life is like cooking; you can use the most wonderful recipe in the world, obtain the finest ingredients possible and follow all the best methods available, but you can't make it done until it's done. Whatever it is you want to accomplish, it just takes the amount of time it takes! You can't rush it or force it. It won't work if you do."

It was infinitely reassuring to hear her repeat that concept; it always added much needed perspective.

Of course, with a cooking recipe there are usually specific time requirements: "Bake for one hour in a preheated oven at 375 degrees." In cooking you know exactly when it's done; you even know before you start the specific amount of time that is needed. In *Life*, the best "recipes" most often don't come with time specifications. And even more confusing, it seems to take different people varying amounts of time to get there, to be "done" or even to recognize when they have achieved what they've been striving for. The big kicker in *Life* is that you never are "done" anyway; there's always more…. more to learn, more to lose, more room for growth…

For many years after graduating from college, I would have a recurring dream that many people say they also frequently have:

> I would arrive in a classroom to take a final exam. I would have no memory of ever taking or attending the class and was always totally unprepared. I would know nothing about the subject matter and have no idea who the professor was. There was always a sense of extreme panic and the clear knowledge that I would fail.

After years of the recurring dream and more importantly, after the challenge of breast cancer, one night the dream was distinctly different from all the previous ones.

> The professor was a therapist whom I knew well and respected tremendously. When I looked at the exam, even though I had never attended the class and did not know the subject matter, I was calm yet full of enthusiasm. The questions on the exam were intriguing and I wanted to learn the information that was required to answer them. I went up to the professor and told her what a wonderful exam she had given. I shared with her my excitement and my goal of reading all of the required books to be able to answer the questions.

With that dream came a totally new feeling and awareness. I could learn whatever I needed to learn. It also didn't matter if I ever took the exam or passed the course. Learning was the alluring and appealing key, rather than getting credit for a class. In the dream, I left the classroom quite sure that I would learn what I wanted and needed to know because I was interested, capable and aware of how to gain the knowledge.

After that new version of the "Being Unprepared for a Final Exam Dream", the recurring dream completely discontinued. Several years passed without any dreams of the end of the semester panic. Shortly after I had begun to pour myself into writing about my experiences with breast cancer, overcoming loss and celebrating life, the dream reappeared in yet another incarnation:

> When I arrived in the classroom there was no professor present to please or to disappoint. The exam was to write a ten-page essay on any topic I wanted. It did not even matter if I had ever attended the class. I was ecstatic since I was totally prepared to take the exam. I knew what I wanted to write and I knew all that I needed to do so. There was a sense of concern because I had arrived late and all the other students had already

> begun writing. I was worried about having enough allotted time left to write what I wanted to say. There was also the challenge of finding paper to write on. It seemed quite important to find unlined white paper. I looked everywhere for paper and found only a few sheets of yellow lined legal pad paper or paper that was already written on. My determination was enormous and without limits to find clean empty freeing paper and to bring my voice to the page.

The evolution of these dreams clearly represented the evolution of my life. That third version dream revealed how ready and confident I was to tell my story. My arriving late to that class reflected my concern about turning to writing at a later stage in life. It also demonstrated how compelled I was to spend every minute focused on writing and delivering my message to the world. The need for unlined white paper indicated my desire to free myself of confining and rigid traditions. Writing within the lines and living within the box would impede my need for control, my need for autonomy, my need for unlimited expression.

For years I had been striving to "get it right", to "fix everything". I saw the loss of my breasts and the loss of powerful and loving relationships with men as huge prices I had paid to learn and grow. It always felt like I was in Oz and needed to get home again. There were even small pictures and actual replicas of Dorothy's red shoes in my house.

The night before I had that most evolved dream was Halloween. Few children if any ever came to my New York City home for trick or treating but I still had my country witch hanging on my front door and my basket of Reese's Cups and Butterfingers waiting anyway. And who should appear to ring my bell? It was none other than a little neighbor dressed as Dorothy, of course. Her tiny shoes were covered with sparkling red fabric. After giving her some candy, I took her to my bulletin board to show her my red shoes and promised to look for my red shoe key ring to give to her as a present if I could find it. She played with my three-pound butterfly dog. If Toby, my son's childhood cairn terrier, had still been alive, I would have let her take "our Toto" with her on her costumed candy quest. When her mother said it was time to leave, she pleaded, "No, I don't want to go; I want to stay here!"

So on Halloween after a visit from a three-year-old Dorothy – so reminiscent of my own vividly looming internal child - I would dream my dream and finally know, like Dorothy, that I had always had the power to be home whenever I wanted. Yet I still recognized that without all of my learning experiences along life's Yellow Brick Road, there would have had to be, continued painful longing, unanswered questions and unwanted neediness.

Being fully engaged in life – putting in time, going through loss, paying attention – can bring rich awareness, astonishing insight and tremendous calm. Maturity and wisdom come from deeply experiencing and fully participating in living. They do not come to those who simply mark time or remain on the sidelines. It takes time to heal; it takes time to gain perspective; it takes time to learn what is needed; it takes time to find the answers; it takes time to become "done".

It felt like I was moving towards living into the answers rather than just appreciating life's questions. It felt like I was finally going to be *done.*

What Comes From Pain

> *"There is a curious paradox that no one can explain.*
> *Who understands the secret of the reaping of the grain?*
> *Who understands why spring is born out of winter's*
> *laboring pain?*
> *Or why we all must die a bit before we grow again?"*
> **The Fantasticks**

Out of pain comes much wonder.

Labor and childbirth provide the most painful experience a woman can endure. Yet the reward of that agony far outweighs the hurt. To feel life moving within you and to see your infant immerge from your body and take life's first breath are miraculous events. As females, we are supremely privileged to be able to carry new life in our wombs and to know, through our suffering, the true value of the miracle of birth. From the first moment we bring a baby into the world, we are radically transformed.

The loss of my breasts generated more personal development than any experience of my life. Like childbirth, the diagnosis of breast cancer dramatically alters who you are. You gain a new identity and your perspectives are forever and dramatically changed. When you lose the most prominent physical symbol of your gender, you must claim your female identity without that symbol.

A deep awareness of my good fortune was significantly magnified for me by my having lost my sister to breast cancer. Instead of thinking "Why me?", I basked in the blessing of my early diagnosis and took on the quest of empowering and informing others and of living life to the fullest.

One night walking home from a Broadway play, I was describing enthusiastically how much I had enjoyed the evening and most probably was nearly skipping down the street. My friend, Jusef, said to me, "You're like a teenager. I've never known anyone as enthusiastic about life as you are." The joy I discover in the

159

simplest events and tasks of everyday living is beyond any I could have possibly experienced without going through my sister's illness and death and my own year of four surgeries.

> It was late October and a man said to me on our elevator ride in the morning, "It sure has turned cold and raw out." My immediate thought, which I expressed, was, "The cold air feels so clean and crisp to me." He thought for a moment and then said, "Yeah, you're right; now it feels refreshing but when February gets here, then it won't seem so great anymore." Without any hesitation, I responded, "Oh, I always love February! The days are getting so much longer again and the light is wonderful." When I realized how I had flipped each of his downtrodden perceptions into something pleasing, I started laughing. "I'm pretty obnoxious with all of my positive thinking, aren't I?" He laughed with me as he stepped off the elevator onto his floor.

There was no question about it. I had become a lemonade maker.

The last remaining area that would finally benefit from my positive perceptions was relationships with men. Often in the past, I had felt used up and hopeless. How could I possibly go out there again, seeking a love partner, a playmate, a soul-friend? Where would I find more feelings? How could I risk *giving* anymore? Eventually and slowly over time, I began to understand fully that *each loss of love expanded my capacity to love*. Rather than shut down and turn off to protect myself from more pain, I came to recognize that every aching loss provided stronger awareness, enhanced vision and greatly enriched growth.

What comes from pain is the gift of true learning. Without pain there cannot be a full appreciation of what is good.

"Deep in December it's nice to remember,
Although you know the snow will follow.
Deep in December it's nice to remember:
Without a hurt the heart is hollow."

The Fantasticks

Cynthia Leeds Friedlander
Surviving Loss

When I was growing up, a favorite pastime at the dinner table was riddles. The harder they were to figure out, the more determined we were to solve them without help from the person who brought the riddle to the table, which usually was my father. My sister and I never let him tell us the answer; we always struggled and struggled until we could figure out the solution.

One of the all-time favorites was:

> **If a train was traveling along the border between the United States and Canada and there was a train wreck directly on the border so that the train and all of the passengers were exactly equally distributed in each country, where would you bury the survivors?**

After letting people debate about all of the issues of citizenship, whether or not there was a way to identify the bodies, etc., etc., someone would of course point out that you don't *bury* survivors.

When corporations downsize their staffs, the people who retain their jobs are referred to as *survivors*. I have always wondered what the label should be for those who are no longer there. Certainly they are often referred to as *terminated*. Who stops to recognize what those words, *survivor* and *terminated*, actually mean and what those two groups experience as they receive and live through those identities?

In natural disasters and grand scale accidents, the reportage that focuses on the survivors always is in contrast to those who did not make it through. When there are survivors, there are usually many that don't survive.

In actuality, the term, survivor, always begs the question. If there are survivors, then who are the non-survivors and what is their designation? It is striking to recognize that the meaning of "survivor" exists only in reference to what no longer exists.

When people label me as a survivor of breast cancer, I have many highly charged reactions:

-I feel guilty claiming that label; my breast cancer was stage zero; there was no threat to my life.
- I suddenly experience the word in contrast to non-survival and feel terrified.
-I forget my jubilance about surviving breast cancer and my joy in living.
-I reject mortality and the categorization of breast cancer *victim.*
-I immediately connect with my sister who did not survive.
-I am so fiercely independent that I reject a word, like survivor, that groups me with others.

We experience our survival in contrast to those who do not survive. A cherished part of my past would soon no longer exist. My steady high school boyfriend had been diagnosed with cancer at age fifty-two. He valiantly fought his attacker but his battle would not be successful. I wrote him a farewell letter:

Dear Cam,

I want to put some thoughts on paper for you ... to bring you comfort ... and to tell you how sad I am that you are going through such hard and horrible times.

It is wonderful to hear what a great attitude you have and to know that your sense of humor is strong and that you are laughing.

As I sit here trying to capture the words I wish to express, I am looking across the room at a photograph of my mother, my sister and me taken when I was around sixteen. The photo was taken by a professional photographer in our living room on Valley Road. It belonged to my grandmother and is in a lovely old frame. My sister had had it in her home and when she died of breast cancer, I got it. Jodie, Mother and I are all three wearing black dresses and the two of them are wearing pearls. I have a delicate gold chain at my neck with a tiny gold heart on it, a gift from you, that I wore always in those days ... do you remember? My sister is a proud young wife and recent mother, full of promise. I am still a girl ... innocent ... happy. My mother is probably eight years younger than I am now. Six very bright black/brown eyes are looking out at me from the past.

... It is good that we cannot see into the future and know what lies ahead. ...

Life has such twists and turns in it and surely it IS the hard stuff that makes us strong and teaches us to appreciate how precious each moment is.

My losses have been big and I long for much that I don't have and still I remain optimistic, happy and see life as a great and wonderful adventure. I feel blessed and know how fortunate I am and how full my life is.

Somewhere in the back of my mind, I have always felt safe, knowing you were in this world. I have always known that if ever I were in trouble or in need that I could turn to you and you would be there for me. It has been a good feeling knowing this, even though our lives are very separate.

Of course, the lesson we must all learn is that safety is an illusion. And self-reliance is the only sure bet we can make. Know that I am fine, that my self-sufficiency is the best gift to come out of my divorce and later breast cancer. Know that I will be okay and that you are a part of who I am. To this day I find myself with pen in hand writing out the jeweler's monogram that was on your grandfather's signet ring you asked me to wear as a symbol of our love. The ring may be long gone but I still hold the monogram, etched forever in my mind and heart.

I want to warn that innocent young girl staring back at me across the room but she can't hear me ... and what would I say to her if she could?

-Be brave.
-Make each day count.
-Cherish and be good to those who love you.
-Protect your body -- respect it, care for it -- you only get one.
-Have fun.
-Take risks.
-Give back to the world.
-Work hard.

Well, maybe she can hear me.

Always,
Cindy

Ultimately, healthy survival is about trust, trust in oneself first of all and secondly trust in those with whom you form bonds and connections. When one experiences the blows of life – cancer diagnoses, divorce, heartbreak – trust is often hard to capture and survival seems threatened.

When a breast cancer survivor going through a painful personal separation sent me an e-mail asking, "How do you ever learn to trust again?"

I responded:

> Trust is a gift you give yourself that others receive the benefits of ... and it takes time. Healing takes time! Be patient with yourself but be demanding too! This is about **CHOICES**. You can choose to shut down, turn off, trust no one, take no prisoners ... or you can choose to
>
> > *-Forgive, forget and live in the present (the hardest of all sometimes).*
> >
> > *-Learn to accept others for who they are – rather than want them to be different from who they are.*
> >
> > *-Concentrate on providing for yourself so that you are whole and self-sufficient so that you don't come together with others out of need and mistrust but rather out of desire and openness.*
> >
> > *-Understand that hurt and heartache are growthful and enriching ... that is not to say that we should be masochistic, seek pain and punish ourselves but rather KNOW that without pain we cannot take in and understand what is truly joyous.*
> >
> > *-Realize that trusting yourself is the key to trusting others. Working on you and understanding the real motivations behind your responses and reactions (which often requires professional outside help) will lead to trusting others.*
> >
> > *-Take risks; without risk-taking there's no potential for development. Take measured and attainable (not guaranteed) risks. It's scary but oh so satisfying once you do. And it won't*

> *always turn out the way you want it to. ...*
> *That's life!*
>
> Anne Frank said, "No matter what, I still believe that
> people are really good at heart." Those words deeply
> struck me when I first read them at age eleven and no
> matter what, I still believe them. Life is good! It's
> hard to trust if you don't believe that.

Being a survivor means being alive when others have lost their
lives. Being a survivor brings a wonderful obligation to give back
to the world and pay homage to those who did not survive.

*Surviving loss and understanding its value is the best
teacher on the planet and is a glorious gift to be highly
cherished and respected.*

Just Be Yourself

After years of living a single life and of being in relationships with men that did not lead to the partnered life I sought, I decided to ask a dear man who was married to my best friend from childhood, to help me look at what I was doing and what I needed to change about myself.

"You have known me for a while and have seen me in a few relationships with different men. I want to hear your perspective on what you see me doing that isn't working or is contributing to why I keep ending up alone."

"Cindy, you're not doing anything wrong. It isn't about doing things right or wrong! It's about being true to who you are. You just need to keep on being yourself and believing in yourself. The best possible thing you can do is just be you."

Gifts come from a large variety of places and in a wide range of forms. That response was a glorious gift that I would always be grateful for. Everyone was talking about *The Rules.* I certainly was too seasoned, independent, confident and free-spirited to be following anybody's rules other than my own. And if I had any of my own, they would be constantly changing anyway. Yet somehow I still thought that there was a formula I should be trying or an approach that I needed to learn about. As spontaneous, natural and untraditional as I was, it was unlikely that I would have been able to adapt to a formula or approach if my friend's husband had given me one.

There are many occurrences that can produce weighty stress and attack self-confidence and I had had my share of them:
>   -Divorce
>   -Death of a sibling
>   -Breast cancer
>   -Double mastectomy
>   -Job loss
>   -Break-up of significant relationships

Following that conversation in which I was told, "Just be yourself." I stopped worrying about what I needed to do or be and I simply started TO BE.

I had always known that the relationships I was in were missing ingredients that were extremely important to me. All I needed to change was being true to those ingredients and the rest would follow. Whether I became coupled or remained uncoupled, I knew who I was and what I wanted.

The giving was the most important part in a relationship but if I didn't give to myself first, there was nowhere left to go.

Cynthia Leeds Friedlander
New York, New York

It was a clear November late afternoon. It had been exactly five
years since the last of four surgeries to remove and reconstruct my
breasts, following a breast cancer diagnosis. I was running beside
the East River heading north, when the Empire State Building
suddenly came into view, over to the northwest, as I rounded the
curve of the river. The sky was a polished and pallid, just-before-
dusk, silver blue. There were feathery pink clouds floating behind
The Empire State Building that were starting to turn gray in the
early evening sky. Along the horizon there was a band of palest
aquamarine to outline the skyline of Queens in the eastern sky and
surprisingly a ribbon of lavender pink just above that.

Ever since I had taken an old friend from Virginia to the top of the
Empire State Building in early June and fallen in love with him
there, that building had taken on a whole new identity for me.
Walking everywhere in the City, I would catch a glimpse of it and
smile.

As I continued my run along the river, the dim sky deepened into a
pure rich blue. The top needle of the Empire State Building was lit
up in yellow lights and below that was a section of red ones.
These two autumnal colors, set off by the brilliant blue sky, made
an unbelievable display of primary color to delight the senses.

I had definitely come to appreciate in recent months that
building's reputation as a phallic symbol and as I ran and took in
the grandeur of the city I lived in, I thought to myself, "It isn't a
phallic *symbol*; it is just simply phallic!" No sooner had I had that
agreeable thought than the elegant Chrysler Building slipped out
from behind the buildings that were hiding it from my view and I
immediately saw its beautiful glistening curving layers setting off
a feminine contrast against the bigger coarser Empire State
Building. As I engaged in my fantasies of those male and female
genital images dominating the New York City skyline, my
imagination wandered to the World Trade Center's paired towers
and I soon identified them as the breasts of my city. They are
mammary and Partonesque in their dominance – solid and

170

welcoming, captivating the eye's attention by their protrusion into view.

These images were entertaining me immensely and spurring on my running pace when I suddenly realized that the very day of my bilateral mastectomy surgery, to remove both of my breasts in February of 1993, was the day of the World Trade Center bombing! Just like the assault on my breasts that day, there was a severe attack on the World Trade Center towers. They too required serious reconstruction and there was also quite an extended period afterwards before things could return to normal again. Most importantly, just as very few people lose their lives as a result of the type of breast cancer I had - unlike other more virulent or more advanced forms of breast cancer - there fortunately was no massive loss of life associated with that 1993 World Trade Center bombing, quite unlike the typical fatality numbers that occur from a bombing like that. It was quite amusing, yet almost eerie, to link all of these images and events together, but there was an even more haunting association to follow in my awareness.

The day of my breast removal surgery and the day of the World Trade Center bombing incident was also the day when the front page top left headline of The New York Times boldly announced that women under the age of fifty may not benefit from mammography. It was infuriating and shocking to see that headline on the same day that I was having my breasts removed. My breast cancer had been identified by mammography only, when I was forty-six years old. It was microscopic and non life-threatening and could never have been diagnosed at such an early stage without mammography. Mammography had provided a way for me to make a radical and dramatic decision to remove both of my breasts so that I would never face another diagnosis of breast cancer again and so that I would never suffer the torment and death that my sister had endured just months prior.

Those who continued on to the second page of that article, hidden within the depths of the newspaper, could read, if they chose to read all the details, that mammography was still the only means to detect certain microscopic breast cancers and that mammography still provided the best means possible of early detection of breast cancer. The fact that the denser breasts of younger women could sometimes make reading mammography difficult, would certainly not be a reason for women under the age of fifty to choose not to have mammograms. My breasts were extremely dense and mammography had still been a means to identify the breast cancer in my breast.

Many of the studies, on which the headlines and conclusions were grounded, came from dated information or were simply based on a bell curve of statistics. Some insurance companies were still refusing to pay for mammography. From an economical and statistical point of view, there may have been a considerable amount of support for not recommending mammography to women under the age of fifty. As an individual woman with my particular set of circumstances, there would have been no way for me to follow the precept of the article. Yet I knew that many women, who were terrified of breast cancer and fearful of the results that mammography might provide them, would choose not to get mammograms as a result of that headline. It would feed their fear and their ignorance. I was enraged and motivated more than ever to become vigilant in my crusade to make sure that woman were fully informed and able to make wise and beneficial decisions about their bodies.

As I ran home across Thirty-Fourth Street, I looked up at the Empire State Building and felt greatly inspired to continue to tell my story and to send out messages to women, to warn them about and protect them from the potentially lethal decisions that many of them were making.

Postscript, Fall 2001: *Four years after I wrote this homage to the New York skyline, my city became Breastless too. The World Trade Center towers fell from terrorist attack on September 11, 2001, changing forever lives and life throughout the world.*

Vigilance

ever vigilant i stand against the world and all its dragons

i know i can take them on and win

they have sneaked up on me and terrified me in the dark

but i will keep the light on so they cannot come from shadowed places

i will shine beacons out to weaken and destroy them

i will find the demons in their infancy before they gather strength

i will warn the unknowing so that badness is diminished

until the death of evil i will build my fortress from the storm

this is a promise to my sister so that her soul can rest in peace

my vigilance is a gift of gratitude for my life

ever vigilant i stand out in the world and all its splendor

i know i can experience unlimited abundance

there is no end to happenings of wonder

and i will walk out in the light to feel the glory of this life

i will shine beacons out to strengthen all my powers

i will find the enchanters in their infancy before they gather wisdom

i will nurture them so that we can become united in delight

until the magnification of goodness i will build golden bridges to the sky

this is a promise to my sister who missed the richness of her old age

my vigilance is a gift of gratitude for my life

Epilogue

Full Circle 2012 - 2013

Two childhood friends had pleaded with me to attend our 48th high school reunion in May of 2012. My mother's 95th birthday celebration had been scheduled three weeks prior and the thought of turning around and driving back to The Star City so quickly after that big party I had thrown for my mother seemed like way too much even to begin to consider. In addition to driving more than seven hours each way from New York and back, I had to remain in New York on Thursday prior to the reunion weekend and had also scheduled a business commitment in New York that couldn't be changed for 8:00 AM on Monday morning following the reunion weekend. Gail had begged on the phone from Utah, almost in tears, "Ohhhhhh, you have to go to the reunion. We haven't seen each other for over eight years. It just won't feel right if you aren't there." Marilyn had just been in New York with me for a ten-day visit so there was less urgency in her plea but she had encouraged so many people to be there and somehow between the two of them I was tempted enough to get my act together and get there in time for the first reunion party on Friday night. There were four classes celebrating high school reunions that weekend: the graduating classes from 1962 through 1965, the first four graduating classes from the back-then, newly-built, city-wide high school.

Friday night's reunion events were four separate parties for each of the four individual classes and ours was in a restaurant down on the City Market. There I was in a sea of seniors thinking how very out of place I felt and thinking how strange it was that I had arrived somewhat on time and neither Marilyn nor Gail were anywhere to be seen. The women all looked fabulous and young; the men, for the most part, looked old and decrepit.

Across the room, I saw a very tall handsome man whom I didn't recognize at all. I immediately thought he had to be a former classmate's husband. I decided to go over to him to check out who he was and to my surprise he was a classmate, Barry K., and one of Marilyn's best friends from high school whom she had also coerced into coming. We clicked right away, not remembering if we had ever even spoken when we were in high school together. Barry had seen a photo of ten of our classmates including me who had had a girl's elementary school mini-reunion two years prior. I had posted the photo from that day on our high school reunion's website. Barry told me he had shown that photo to some of his friends at work and had asked them what age they thought the women were in the photo. His friends had all thought we were probably in our early forties. I immediately high-fived Barry when he told me that and Barry later told me there was such a twinkle in my eyes at that moment that he had immediately fallen in love with me. It was a fun evening and we ended up in groups moving from reunion party to reunion party. I attended three of the four parties, purposefully skipping the class of 63's party in a private home to avoid running into my old heartbreaker Jesse in case he was going to be there.

By the end of the second night of the reunion Barry had become a man on a mission. When I left the hotel ballroom to go retrieve my car to go home to my mother's to get some good sleep for my drive back to New York the next day on Sunday, Barry grabbed my hand and walked me down the majestic hotel staircase through the grand lobby. When the valet brought out my car, Barry got in the passenger seat and asked me to pull around to talk before I drove away.

As he was talking in the passenger seat, I suddenly saw my father's face right there in front of me. The whole weekend had passed without my seeing that this man looked so much like my father, it was way beyond spooky. As our relationship unfolded after that reunion weekend, every one of my friends and family members who met Barry or saw pictures of him immediately saw this striking resemblance. For sure I was swept away by him and all that he represented in my fantasy image of what I wanted in a man and what felt to me to be missing from my life up until then. For sure I had adored my father more than life itself and had said before he died that I didn't want to be in the world if he were no longer in it. I drove away from that reunion, floating. How delicious to be floating at sixty-six years of age! Barry pursued and wooed. And I was simply swept away. Our connection somehow had a life and momentum all its own and for the next six months it definitely felt like the real deal.

Barry read my Breastless manuscript and was moved to tears. He encouraged me to get it published and make it happen. His mother had died of breast cancer when he was in his twenties and he was enthralled by my breast cancer story that was so magnificently different from his mother's. Her story was much more like my sister's. Barry and I discovered that unaware we had lived in the same apartment complex for the first three years of our lives. We discovered that we were born in the same hospital. We found out that we had shared the same pediatrician. There was this sense of how much we were meant to be together and for a while I ignored how extremely different our political beliefs were, how different our body clocks were, how different our lifestyles and personal preferences were. Eventually things started to fall apart, little by little in many different ways; by the end of January it was clearly over.

Here's the vignette I wrote looking back the following February.

> *I feel like I'm supposed to have figured it all out by now. I know that WRITING is my truest place. I'm staring at the keyboard and see it as my ally and my enemy. I feel my word gifts flowing from my fingertips onto the keys and still feel mocked by ineptitude. I have been intimately close to Hadley and Hemingway in recent days, reading The Paris Wife followed by The Moveable Feast. I devoured both books. I became simultaneously inspired and daunted; these opposing pulls could have canceled each other out and stifled my desire to write. Somehow though I am compelled - the keyboard is my paintbrush, the screen my canvas. I am listening to my muse, I am*

watching the words fill the page; I keep typing.

As I was reading about Hem through Hadley's eyes when they lived in Paris and then read his memoir of that same timeframe, I recognized more and more that greatness in art is elusive and obtainable by few. It also became clear that the act of writing is one of discipline and motivation above all else. It's about fighting for the words and claiming them in one's own voice. It's always about truth. It's truth that I pursue rather than the achievement of greatness through writing. And yet I want to be profound. I want my writing to be elegant, and fresh. I want to touch the world with meaning. I want to find the metaphors that represent life that will resonate for others. I know I am a wordsmith; I want to be a real writer.

Being on the first edge of the Boomer generation feels like a sick circus. Mick Jagger still strutting like a boy, Cher chasing that illusive body image and high cheekbone chiseled face, there seems to be a misfit between what my flower generation espouses, how it sees itself, and the reality of the life stage we have all fallen into finally. I have always heard older women describe their experience of themselves as feeling like they're still the same girls they've always been. Their wrinkled faces and aching widening bodies have betrayed their inner experience of themselves. And the Botox and cosmetic surgery, that are so readily available to them, magnify the futility of their beliefs and pursuits.

Except for the tightness and ache in my neck and shoulders when I sit hunched over the keyboard writing, my body still feels quite girl-like; I am pain-free and active. I run up and down stairs the same way as always. I'm still the same athletic nimble-bodied thin woman I have always been. Anyone who hears me state my age is always shocked. I look much younger than I am and feel much younger in every way. The only cosmetic surgery I have experienced is the surgery to reconstruct my missing breasts that were simultaneously removed more than twenty years ago after a non life-threatening diagnosis of stage zero carcinoma in situ, three months following the death of my only sister from advanced metastatic breast disease. My energy stays astoundingly abundant and available, like that silly pink rabbit in those annoying battery commercials.

Definitely, I feel the passing of time through other ways than my youthful physicality and limitless energy. I have faced many challenges and disappointments; I'm frequently sad and often emotionally fatigued. I had so wanted a break and thought I'd finally earned one, that I'd finally gotten it right. I met Big B at my 48th high school reunion in the spring and our whirlwind experience has left me lost again. It doesn't seem possible that eight months ago I was floating and sure.

Across a crowded room, just like the song lyrics describe, it seemed like my enchanted evening had finally occurred. We met; we clicked; we connected; we became one. And just as spontaneously, serendipitously and swiftly as it began and unfolded, eight months later it has vanished. In spite of gazillions of adoring phone calls and texts; in spite of hours and hours of days and nights together sharing, cooking, talking, eating, reading, sleeping, swimming, biking, kissing, hugging, driving, sightseeing; in spite of vows of everlasting love and commitment without ambivalence; despite all this, it has disappeared.

There were many words spoken; there were understandings mapped out repeatedly; there were beliefs and desires reinforced and cemented in place. And then there was no delivery, no money where the mouth was, no cushion or safe haven to support the empty words. And so ... poof! All those elated emotions have vanished like cotton candy on the tongue, leaving a sweet residue for a short while and then nothing. The emptiness is unbearable, it hurts like hunger. And like hunger, it creates the drive for sustenance, nourishment, self-protection and, above all, self-sufficiency.

Recently, in a doctor's office, the surgeon's business manager asked me, "How's that beautiful relationship going with the man from your reunion?" I shared the true and sad unwinding of events as simply and succinctly as I could and she wrapped it all up, saying, "So he told you what you wanted to hear, right?"

I clean, I cook, I reach out for work and fulfillment. I lick my wounds and seek comfort. What also comes with this disappointment are acute bursts of motivation and ever-present deep, deep longing. What is this elusive place I seek, this calm and sureness that is glimpsed, deeply felt and yet never endures? I thought I had found it. It all seemed right. It all seemed earned. It felt like I had arrived. I look at these questions and see the shocking truth. True serenity can only come from within and cannot be dependent on a relationship or external and material gains. How many times is this lesson going to be presented before I am actually on the other side? What I am glimpsing is so evident yet elusive, like Dorothy and her ruby red shoes. We are all always home, if we can stop our pursuit to become and simply

BREATHE THE PRESENT *and* EMBRACE THE NOW.

One year after the reunion, I can look back with great gratitude for all that I learned in the most profound way in these last twelve months. I have gained so much and am full of positive feelings; I have expanded understanding of life's joys and challenges, its hardships and demands; I am full of youthful passion to engage in life fully and respectfully, with great compassion and empathy. And I am forever indebted to Barry who will always be my dear, dear friend. He took me where I needed to go to be able to see all that was right and good in my life, to see that the missing elements I was looking for were actually very superficial and unimportant and that what I most wanted in life and from a relationship, I already had.

I traveled significantly on life's road during the past year and experienced three extraordinary journeys:

1-the full circle through breast implant replacement surgery, revisiting my double mastectomy and reconstruction experiences from twenty years prior,

2-the full circle back to the deepest truest love of my life, the prior relationship I had heartlessly abandoned to be with Barry,

and finally

3-the full circle of emotional and psychological growth and rebirth.

Full Circle 1

Around 10:00 PM on Friday, August 17, 2013, I was on the phone with Barry, walking around my bedroom. I had been simultaneously trying on clothes to decide which ones I wanted to purge from my overflowing closets. Suddenly I observed a very strange and troubling image as I passed in front of the mirror over the low chest of drawers across from my bed. I blurted out in great shock, "Sh##! Something is wrong!" My right saline-filled breast implant was collapsing. It was leaking internally and had caved in on the top and was no longer firm and bowl shaped. It was horrifying to see this happening after twenty years. Even though I was actually breastless and had been for all this time, my breast implant reconstruction surgery had been simultaneous with my bilateral breast removal mastectomy surgery and I had never been without either two matching real breasts or two matching artificial breast implants. I had seen my sister's natural breast next to her implanted one and that sight had contributed tremendously to my decision to have both breasts removed and reconstructed all those years ago. It was unsettling and disturbing beyond any feelings I could have imagined I would feel in those circumstances. Because it had been such a long time, I had become completely accustomed to my body and the unnatural shape of the saline-filled implants. I had become cocooned in my little world of normalcy, thinking I looked just fine and that I would never experience a failed implant or want to have newer more natural-looking breast implants.

That weekend dragged on interminably as I waited for Monday morning to call my breast surgeon's office. I was extremely fortunate because his office was being renovated at that time and he had no patients scheduled at all. Because of my emergency situation, and his lack of appointments altogether, he agreed to come into the office to see me the very next day – Tuesday, August 21. By the time that appointment was over, I had been scheduled for dual implant replacement surgery - with the new and improved, safe, much more naturally shaped, silicone gel breast implants - exactly eight days later on August 29.

Those eight days were full of emotion. Each day, I awoke with a more depleted, more deformed right breast as the saline fluid continued to leak inside my body. I was sure that I could smell its rotten stench coming from my pores. Whether it was real or imaginary, that smell would disappear completely as soon as the surgery took place. It was a pressured timeframe. There were pre-op medical appointments. There were antibiotics and holistic herbal products to purchase. There were arrangements to be made. There were details to be taken care of.

It was striking how reconnected I became to the faded events of 1992, the year when my sister died of advanced virulent breast cancer that had metastasized to her brain and when I received my stage-zero, non life-threatening diagnosis of ductile carcinoma in situ. All of the many past surgeries and cancer-related experiences came back into view and focus. Also the awareness of my blessings was once again reinforced. At the age of 66 with a new high-school-reunion boyfriend, I was going to get lovely new breasts. I was going to have surgery. I was going to be new and improved. I was going to experience all of this without illness or life threat.

The surgery went well and I came home with drains under each of my new breasts. Barry and I measured the fluids in those drains as instructed twice a day and even after he had returned to North

Carolina, he was on the phone with me as I measured the drain
fluids, supporting each step toward recovery from surgery. My
new breast implants looked and felt much more like real breasts
than the old saline implants ever had. I announced with great
pride that I wanted to go skinny dipping which was an activity I
had certainly never done in the prior twenty years with my
unnatural-looking saline implants.

After twenty years, my mastectomy and breast reconstruction were
simply part of my history and part of who I was. Being in a new
relationship could have made the implant failure and the implant
replacement surgery very difficult, uncomfortable and even
embarrassing. Of course, there may be many women who would
have found this experience very challenging to share so openly
and, for sure, there are many men who would not opt to be an
intimate part of this type of medical and physical experience. For
me, I felt totally comfortable sharing it all and for Barry –
particularly because of his own mother's mastectomy and valiant
fight against cancer – he was completely receptive to and
participative in each facet of this medical adventure we shared. I
am grateful to him for that and always will be.

At the first post-op appointment with my surgeon, he showed me
his terribly swollen and tender right forefinger. He told me that
this was caused by the deeply embedded and encapsulated scar
tissue he had to remove when he took out my left still-filled and
intact saline breast implant. That explained why the pain had been
more intense and why the post-surgery drain had always been
much fuller on that left side. He demonstrated in the palm of his
left hand with his painfully swollen right index finger how he had
scooped away the excessive thickened tissue growth from my
chest cavity. It was a graphic and meaningful illustration of what
it takes to remove deep scars that have been embedded for years.

About three weeks after the surgery, I started to see red blotches
on my skin in the area of first one breast and then the second one.
My surgeon prescribed antibiotics and within 48 hours, as the
redness increased, he had me go to the New York Cornell Medical
Center Emergency Room and ended up meeting me there on a late

September Sunday night. My antibiotic prescription was changed several times before an infectious disease specialist put me on high dosages of Dicloxacillin which I stayed on for several months to ensure the complete eradication of infection. The scary element was that the implants could have become contaminated by the infection and it would have become necessary to remove and replace them.

I am still faced with the potential of implant exchange or corrective surgery yet again because of minor capsular contracture, hard fibrous lumps along the top edge of both implants. These can be felt and palpitated easily yet they are not particularly raised or immediately noticeable to the eye. The contours of my breasts are lovely and are much more natural-looking than my old saline implants were. I'm quite happy with them for now. I am concerned that these lumpy areas may expand and even cause discomfort. From the research I've read, this phenomenon is caused by the body's natural tendency to form scar tissue. It is interesting how different this irregularity in internal scarring is from the old original saline implants. Both types of implants are made of the same silicone "containers". I think about being 80 years old and facing a similar dilemma to the one I experienced this past year. Would I just have them removed and be done with breasts forever? Who knows if I'll make it to 80 or be facing that question then! For now I am content and alive. For now I am healthy. For sure, my breasts look better at 66 than they did at 46. For sure, it's quite satisfying to be at the age of old and droopy and instead look fresh, young and perky.

My surgeon is nonchalant and generous about my facing yet another surgery. Because I was originally a cancer patient of his twenty years ago for my original reconstructive surgeries, he did not charge me for this current surgery and care, and would not charge me if there is a decision to correct the capsular contracture. I don't ever want to have any kind of elective surgery. I am terrified of getting yet another hospital-born infection that could be much more serious and deadly than the one I so recently experienced. And then there is the thought of surgical cutting, potential drains, more scarring and recovery all over again. I am quite happy with my results and very glad to have the surgery behind me and have newly implanted breasts in front of me. My goal is never to have another hospital experience or surgery of any kind, if possible. It would be more than wonderful if I achieve that goal.

Full Circle 2

On March 1, 2002, I met the love of my life. It only took eleven years for me to realize that was true.

Sometimes

sometimes you have to lose to gain

sometimes what is most precious is right in front of you and you can't even see it

sometimes you get a second chance to make up for your wrong-doings

sometimes the lessons are really hard so that you will never forget so that you will never take gifts for granted so that you will always cherish what is real and true

sometimes you get to see the light and know how blessed you are

sometimes it all comes together exactly as it was meant to be

For ten years, I saw so many wonderful traits in Nate that I cherished dearly:
-He was a wordsmith and poet and wrote magnificently; he was word-gifted.
-He adored music and took me to endless fabulous venues and introduced me to magical performers.
-He shared my political and ethical views; we were always on the same page.
-He read voraciously.

-He hated television (like I did) as a constant background accompaniment to life.

-He respected and admired that I had made hard choices and had had my breasts removed.

-He appreciated, believed in and always, always supported my writing.

-He always wanted and encouraged me to get my Breastless memoir published.

-He was a runner, a skier, a tennis player.

-He had strong family values.

-He was a devoted adoring wonderful lover.

-He gave wonderful gifts and was generous in nature and in action.

-He was funny and smart.

-He was aware and in-tune.

-He was intuitive and always got the meaning and signs along the way.

-He loved movies, concerts, theater and cultural centers of all types.

-He was technically with it.

-He always participated fully and gladly in domestic and yard work.

-He adored my friends.

-He was worshipful of me. He doted on me.

-He was thoughtful. He got me. He knew my idiosyncrasies and protected them.

-He was giving and cared about making the world better for the underdog.

-He was fun. He was kind. He was good.

-He was in the world the way I was in the world.

-He had endless energy and matched me in my always being ready to add to the day.

-He was an animal- and nature-lover.

-He and I were in synch, on the same wave length, cared about so many of the same causes.

-He was all that and more.

-… so much more.

So what was missing? So why did I think Big Barry was the answer to my dreams? So how could I have heartlessly turned my back on loving adoring Nate without so much as a look back in regret? How could I have been so blind? All I can say is that there were some unwritten lists in my head of what I felt was wrong and what I thought was missing. There was a list of occurrences that had taken place that felt like ultimate deal breakers. There was a list that felt significant and important, some bizarre sense of entitlement that had to be satisfied by some ideal bigger-than-life image that incorporated my father, Prince Charming and probably some version of a combination of Sean Connery, Ryan Gosling and John F. Kennedy. And if I were a Christian or a religious believer, I'm pretty sure Jesus would have gotten into the mix as well. There was clearly a grand fantasy that could never be satisfied ever. And I believed in it anyway.

Here's how I, thankfully, came full circle back to Nate. Here's how I finally stepped out of the web of expectation and entitlement. Here's how I came to accept and understand my own impediments and blocks, my unquenchable demands, my unattainable relationship requirements, and worst of all my judgments.

Initially, it was just simple longing and missing that took me by surprise. After all I had met my Prince Charming and had quickly (blindly, stupidly, ashamedly) made the ultimate sacrifice and decision to abandon Nate and move ahead full speed with Barry. The reawakening probably first occurred during Hurricane Sandy. I wanted to talk to Nate. I wanted him to call to see if I was okay. I wanted to share New York with him. I missed him. Then there was *The Newsroom* on HBO. Nate had loved Aaron Sorkin's *West Wing*. I knew he would adore this smart timely clever political news series. I wanted to talk to him about it. I couldn't talk to Barry about it. Barry was on another planet from the one I was on politically. I had said it didn't matter. It mattered a lot. I missed being with Nate. I missed being with someone on my same planet. As I came to see that Barry was not going to fulfill the financial commitments he had made to me, I also came to see that the picture I had created of our lives fitting together didn't really exist.

I came out of my blind fantasy and knew clearly and without a doubt that this relationship wasn't working, wasn't going to work, wasn't what I wanted at all.

And each time I saw the mismatch, I also saw the match of Nate. I saw and felt the connection. I deeply felt the love and the loss. I profoundly regretted the painful harm I had caused. I knew that my moving towards Nate could be just a reaction based in panic and that I had severed our bonds so harshly that the damage could be irreparable. I continued to concentrate on rebuilding my life and on being okay on my own. Barry and I, over time, examined together all that we had shared and believed. It was sad and painful and it was also beautiful and growthful. I had thought of Barry as my "bechert", my meant-to-be soul mate. As our relationship came apart, the disappointment was unbearable.

Now looking back, it all still seems meant to be in the most positive way possible. Without Barry, I could have never learned and seen all that I came to be grateful for. I could never have been so appreciative and come to love Nate again as unconditionally and fully as I do now. I actually began to list in my head all the shortcomings and missing pieces that I had legitimized and held onto so intensely over time. I saw each and every one of them in a new light. Even some of the big potentially deal breaker challenges that Nate and I had been through were totally different to me now. I realized that Nate's intent had never been to deceive me. He had kept things from me at certain points in time because of how much he had struggled with them or how uncomfortable he had been with them but certainly not to deceive me. He had shown me that so clearly. And I had "accepted" and gone on with him and moved ahead in spite of the designation of deceit I held onto.

It wasn't real acceptance at all. It wasn't understanding. It wasn't forgiving. I held these shortcomings or mistakes in some accounting system and racked them up like a scorecard of entitlement. I had included occurrences in the accounting stockpile like something as insignificant as standing on tiptoes to appear a bit taller in a photograph. I had seen this innocuous action as vain and superficial and insecure; now it seems endearing, value-neutral, charming and without negative weight at all. And how many times have I sucked in my stomach for a photo? I mean, come on. Really? I have such shame for my shallow disbursement of judgment. Shame and regret and apology. Truly, from the biggest to the smallest item on my unwritten carefully tended lists, I came to see each and every one as insignificant and meaningless. I saw each one disintegrate. I saw the lists disappear. Better still, I saw the need for the lists disappear. I disrobed myself from judgment as if I'd been wearing a cloak of plagues. I felt lighter and loving. I felt accepting and appreciative. I felt apologetic in the deepest sincerest way possible.

As time unfolded I found I was genuinely missing Nate more and more each day. I could feel the depth of love and history between us. I could feel the truth of all that we shared. I could appreciate and adore all of the attributes and characteristics I listed above about him. The more solid these feelings became, the more protective I felt of Nate's feelings. I loved him and wanted him and at the same time I wanted to protect him from me as well. I was the one who had walked away. I was the one with the history of unsatisfied expectations. I was the one with so many judgments. I was the one who had crushed him by turning my back on him.

In early March, I sent Nate a birthday card with a note inside that said,

> *Nate,*
>
> *At some point down the road, I would like to make a time for us to talk – (not write) without anger, accusation or hostility. If that isn't possible/desirable for you, I will understand.*

I want you to know that no matter how differently you experienced it, I always intended to be loving and caring. I apologize for the pain I caused. I apologize that I was so put off by your anger that I could not find any receptivity to your responses and reactions. I have come to appreciate and see many things differently.

True perspective can only come over time.

In truth and with affection,

Cindy

In April, I got a birthday card from him with a letter inside saying,

Cindy,

First of all, thank you for the birthday card and letter, which was totally unexpected.

If you want to talk, we can talk. I would prefer to do it in person, so I can look into your eyes to try and figure out why. I realize that probably won't happen. I will be in NYC for a few days later this month, but my schedule is going to be pretty tight.

Much of the pain you caused has dissipated and in many ways I am stronger for the experience. My life is very full.

191

I hope your new relationship is all that you wanted it to be and that you will celebrate your birthday with a full and happy heart!

Nate

When he came to the City at the end of April, we agreed to meet and talk in my apartment. When he walked in the door, I was so happy to see him I felt like I might burst into light and disappear into the sun. I cried tears of love and tears of regret. I told him I wanted to talk about Acceptance, Appreciation and Apology. I poured my heart out. I told him that he had always told me I was very critical and I said I knew that was true. I said that my being critical was not the problem; I could not like something and that would be okay. I told him that I knew what was not okay was how judgmental I was. I told him how I recognized this and never wanted to be that ever again. I told him everything. I told him that I loved him. I told him about the coming apart of Barry and me.

He told me about a poet who was dying that he had met and had formed such a wonderful relationship with, about how it had helped him heal and move outside of himself; he told me about how beautifully this man had died and what he had gained from this moving experience. He told me about Cathy, the woman he was in a relationship with who was in love with him the way he had been in love with me. He told me that she had just discovered about ten days before that she had a tumor and was having surgery sometime within the next week or so to determine exactly what her situation was.

Our mutual love was palpable and there was so much tenderness and warmth. I could feel how evolved he had become from all that had happened. I knew that he would not sustain a relationship with me for even one brief moment if he glimpsed the slightest indication that I was that woman of judgment he had known before. I knew that I would have to show him proof beyond proof of all that I was telling him. I told him that as sincere as my words were and as much as he could know that sincerity from looking into my eyes and listening to me, that I knew it was about actions and sustaining over time, demonstrating my love over time. I declared to him then and have made it my mantra that I intend to spend the rest of my life showing him how much I love and honor him and how sorry I am for my choices and actions and for the hurt I inflicted.

We spent three and a half hours together. We held each other. We talked. We kissed. I felt his deep love returned to me. He was tender. He was free of anger.

He flew back to Portland, Oregon and to Cathy who has since been diagnosed with very aggressive inoperable cancer. She has started chemotherapy and radiation. They have told her she will be able to participate in a clinical trial. It is very grim.

Nate and I are in regular daily email and text communication and have spoken by phone every week. He writes to me cautiously of love. He sends me carefully chosen love lyrics and romantic YouTube music clips. I feel that he sees and wants our destinies joined together. He is dealing with the most horrific situation with Cathy. I am so concerned about his being able to cope with all that he is facing. The demands on him are extremely high and he does nothing lightly. He does everything with heart. He tells me I am his port in the storm. He tells me I am his heartsong.

I am grateful for all of it. I feel like it is right that I pay a significant price for what I did. I am clear about the importance of my being patient and understanding. I tell myself lovingly that this is the lesson I most needed to learn. Someone can love you with all his heart and still love someone else and still choose to make someone else's needs a higher priority. Love is infinite. Well-being comes from within. True love is unconditional and asks for nothing in return. This is what I feel in the deepest part of my heart.

Here are some of the poems that have poured out of me to send to Nate since that day we first reconnected:

Somewhat

somewhat aware is all i can really be
of the emotional weight you carry
with such grace and devotion

somewhat sufficient is just the starting point
of my apology to you for the pain i've caused you

somewhat fully is all i can achieve
in telling you the measure of what you mean to me

somewhat adequate describes the limitations
in the words that exist to express my love for you

somewhat possible is the potential
for me to ever begin to tell you how much i love you

You

you are my day's first breath

you are my soul's best mate

you are my body's finest touch

you are my life's reason and its heart

you

Heartsong

my heartsong sings for only you
lilting through each day on wings of joy

my heartsong pours out dedicated promise
ringing loudly true love's pure infinity

my heartsong is my ever present conscience
reminding me of constant care commitment

my heartsong is like sweet ambrosia
arousing deep desire aimed to bring you pleasure

my heartsong is my golden gift to you
leveling all the mountains we will have to climb

Rest Assured

rest assured i come to you brand new

all i ever was transformed

i step forward into new being

cleansed of judgment's need

stripped of first-place top-dog craving

escaped from pedestal's captivity

i still bring youth's eternal charm and grace

filled with joyful glee

ready to embrace life's bounty

schooled with acceptance of life's challenges

engaged and present

loving and open

rest assured

Cynthia Leeds Friedlander
The Gift of Cathy

you are the guiding light whose beacon i must follow
you gave the love to n that i withheld
i will give tribute to you for all my life
my sadness for your illness is consuming

your passing will be forever in my present
to keep me on the path i pledge to follow
your life will illuminate the way for my awareness
of my past
full of transgression
of my future
forever in your debt
forever honoring eternal love for n

you are the lesson that i had to learn
you are the payment that i gladly pay
you are the example of grace for which i give thanks
you will always be the inspiration that i honor

i came back to n through
true love and longing
appreciation, acceptance and apology
recognition of all that he is that i had blindly
diminished, ignored and abandoned

it is you that renders all my desire
true and steadfast
worthy and real
deserved and hard-won

thank you for your teaching
thank you for cherishing n
thank you for the love lessons
necessary for healing
necessary for reuniting
necessary for true love's
balance and fulfillment

thank you for the gift of you

Someday

someday beckons with shining promise

someday provides future's hope

someday is just around the corner

someday is reward for patience

someday fills beliefs with calm

someday is within reach

someday will come to light the way

i pledge my someday to you

In looking at and appreciating all that was and will be between Nate and me, I have come to see such significance that I never fully recognized before now. I dream of being with Nate again in the truest, most unconditionally loving relationship possible. I yearn to be with him intimately. It is with great irony that I value so much of our history that I was blind to in the past. When Nate and I began having an intimate relationship in 2002, of course there was a point in time when I told him about my bilateral mastectomies and my implants. At whatever moment that was, it was shared with total ease and comfort. Even though the specifics of what was said, where we were or when exactly I gave this information to him, are long gone from my memory, I can say with certainty that when that communication took place, I was completely relaxed and without apprehension.

There followed quite a series of significant obstacles in our intimate life together that we overcame. What I cherish above all else are the sensations that I could experience vicariously with Nate through his impassioned sensitivity to nipple stimulation which he adored and I no longer could enjoy for myself since I was without natural nipples. This loving special intimacy is yet another element, like so many Nate and I shared, that I see now in retrospect how much I treasure and for which I had little

197

recognition of the importance that this sweetness held for me until it was gone. I am thankful every day for our reconnection and for the tender future that lies ahead for us.

Full Circle 3

"Be patient toward all that is unsolved in your heart and try to love the questions themselves... Do not now seek the answers, which cannot be given you because you would not be able to live them. And the point is, to live everything. Live the questions now. Perhaps you will then gradually, without noticing it, live along some distant day into the answers."

Rainer Maria Rilke

The past year's full circle of emotional and psychological growth and rebirth has taken me to levels I have always sought yet only glimpsed longingly all my life. I have carried Rilke's words in my head and in my heart. I have lived the questions diligently and whole-heartedly. It is with great satisfaction that I see myself living now into the answers. The unrest I have always experienced is calmed. I am at ease. I am content.

Even though my old saline-filled hardened encased unnatural breast implants had become acceptable and normal to me, the rupture of one of them required replacement surgery that brought me once again into another realm of awareness and a new experience of my body. The implant failure was shocking and abrupt yet took me on a journey to a brighter better place. Now I have softer, more natural looking breasts that even jiggle a little like real breasts do and I am, once again, forever changed. I can even appreciate the irregularity from the capsular contracture where I can place my hand and feel the ropey hardness just below the surface of my skin that serves as a reminder for all I've lost and all I've learned.

Full Circle

full circle gives me calm
  showing me the truth of life

full circle gives me vision
  building strength to carry through

full circle releases guilt
  guiding me to paths of light

full circle frees my need
  emptying judgment's dungeon

full circle takes me high
  finding glory and fulfillment

I feel like I've finally figured it all out. I feel like I'm a woman transformed. I see that to be truly alive means constant struggle and growth. The never-ending teachings are always there. It's how you cope that matters most and what you take away from life's unending lessons.

It is my dearest hope that all I have shared on these pages, representing my origins and over twenty years of my life, will be a cherished gift for those who are facing challenging decisions about their bodies, their health, their relationships and their intimacies. I wish for others the support and love I've had over the years and the strength and inner confidence to know that ...

Well-being always comes from within.

www.ingramcontent.com/pod-product-compliance
Lightning Source LLC
LaVergne TN
LVHW091253080426
835510LV00007B/250